T0273115

REIN GOLD

Elfriede Jelinek, who was born in 1946 and grew up in Vienna, now lives in Vienna and Munich. She has received numerous awards for her literary works, which include not only novels but also plays, poetry, essays, translations, radio plays, screenplays and opera librettos. Her awards include the Georg Büchner Prize and the Franz Kafka Prize for Literature. She was awarded the Nobel Prize in Literature in 2004 for her 'musical flow of voices and counter-voices in novels and plays that, with extraordinary linguistic zeal, reveal the absurdity of society's clichés and their subjugating power'.

Gitta Honegger was previously Professor of Theatre at Arizona State University and Professor of Dramaturgy and Dramatic Criticism at the Yale School of Drama. She also served as the resident dramaturg and stage director at the Yale Repertory Theatre. Translations from German include plays by Elfriede Jelinek, Thomas Bernhard, Peter Handke, Peter Turrini, Marieluise Fleißer, Elias Canetti and others. Her work has been supported by several grants, including a Guggenheim and a Fulbright/IFK Fellowship.

'In *rein GOLD*, Jelinek reimagines the characters of Brünnhilde and Wotan from Wagner's Ring cycle and transposes them into the context of modernity. She delivers an impassioned exposé of the discontents of capitalism. Her musical thought is interwoven with myth, politics, and Wagnerian motifs. Gitta Honegger's excellent translation allows us to experience the intense flow of her characters' streams of conciousness entangled in greed and alienation.'
— Xiaolu Guo, author of *A Lover's Discourse*

'*rein GOLD* is a masterful, obsessional, hypnotic journey. Jelinek brings a sharp modernity and relevance to a series of inward wanderings. She is equal to a great myth and makes it new.'
— A.L. Kennedy, author of *The Little Snake*

'Living legend Elfriede Jelinek's *rein GOLD*, rhapsodically written from the maw of forlorn gods, echoes like an incensed dialogue-eulogy designed to fill the space soon left behind the eventual implosion of the twenty-first century's bottomless appetite for capital, for absent love. "For what?" *rein GOLD*'s Brünnhilde asks and asks, trying out answers like mad masks, in search of something lost out here among us that even the gods cannot quite name, yet found as if alive here for all to feel – as in the masterworks of Bernhard's *Correction* and Lispector's *The Passion According to G.H.* – by the inimitable, majestically incensed end-visions of master Jelinek.'
— Blake Butler, author of *Alice Knott*

'Jelinek's work is brave, adventurous, witty, antagonistic and devastatingly right about the sorriness of human existence, and her contempt is expressed with surprising chirpiness: it's a wild ride.'
— *Guardian*

Fitzcarraldo Editions

REIN GOLD

ELFRIEDE JELINEK

Translated by
GITTA HONEGGER

B: Brünnhilde
W: Wotan, the Wanderer

B: I am trying to state the following more precisely,
that's a somewhat delicate area, it is difficult for me. So
then. Papa had this fortress built for him and now he
can't repay the credit. A situation as in any other family.
The remains of tools and machines have been cleared,
the giants used those backhoe arms of theirs, which
surely was not in keeping with their original daydreams.
And what did they get for it? What was their accom-
plishment? What was their payment? Sure, they figured
that other wanderers will be up and about there, shameless wayfarers, uhm, waylayers of the law. The giants
will be last when it comes to paying. Holding out their
hands they will have been first. It won't do them any
good. Why should they return what someone else stole?
What's free for the taking, the beautiful woman, why
should they not have her, why shouldn't they make the
most of what they've got? They've got more weight than
others, they are worth their weight in pounds, they don't
need to gain more, either the woman as commodity form
or the woman inside commodity forms. No, the apples
stay here for now, without the gardener no added value
will sprout from them, the exchange value, does anyone
happen to know it? It must be gigantic, if only because
there is nothing that they could compare themselves
with or relate to. For those apples can't be eaten. Gold.
Whoever has it does not return it. Possession is theft.
That is the short version. And that would be the end of
it. The, what's her face, Fricka, the wife, but that's really
all she is, lambasts Papa because of the credit. The mood
in the fortress is unbearable. Arguments. Papa says: But
you wanted the new house! Mama says: I asked you

before, you said you wanted it too. We have to live somewhere, don't we? I must admit I was glad that you
wouldn't be out-of-house so much. Big mistake. We did
not consider the sacrifices it would cost us. The property
lured and who came? Thousands of strange creatures,
all of them making claims. Anyone making claims becomes their slave in turn and already the first one in this
chain was stealing, nonetheless, to steal from a thief is
also theft, Papa. And did you return what you took from
the thief? You must have signed hundreds of IOUs,
Papa! Do you even know, at least approximately, how
much you owe and to whom? Can you still make heads
or tales of it? What about the untimely coincidence of
the fate of your house and your time running out like
milk from a leaky bottle or latte from the paper cup of a
trendy café chain, the final link of which is, as always,
the end-user who pays for it all in the end? Even if he
drops the cup? A new house at favourable terms and
conditions, you just have to pay with a human being who
isn't one in reality or else no one would give a damn
about her – who wouldn't make a grab for her? That's
what you thought. No wonder. There are plenty of humans, but this one comes only once, this goddess, with
what else could the giants be appeased? The pauperized
worker, whom you did not employ, of course and if, then
far below the collective contract, else he would not be a
pauper, you did not want to promise him anything, no,
you'd have never promised him a thing, you ordered
giants right away, who save you all the other workers,
spare you from them, replace them, every giant thousands of workers (even though you, in any case, right
from the start, yes, I can see it: even though you made
sure to write it down, you did not want to stick to any of
it, no contracts, no labour contract, no loan contract, no

marriage contract, that's where it all begins, I'd say!), and those two were the dummies, the giants, dumb before, haven't learned a thing inbetween, dumb thereafter; the universal worker: let's say that one there, a worker like many, just that we got only this one in, one no one sees and hasn't seen in many years, well, you were not about to employ that one, even though he lowered his labour power so far below value that he totally disappeared in the meantime. For years no one has seen a real worker! That's probably why you took the giants, you also promised them something, I am sure, you are constantly promising something, which you don't have to keep. Others would have installed machines, they wouldn't have made any demands, okay, maybe their bosses, but not they! But wherever the machine takes over the field of production, it produces chronic misery amidst the competing labour power, which has disappeared, to fight their fights elsewhere, where else would it be?, they always have to fight for collective agreements, not here, fortunately, but luckily there, in a place they can't be seen, their work should be seen, not they, children should also be seen but not heard, they are like children themselves, it makes no sense to employ them, there are far too many, everywhere and gone, withdrawn from us, and on top of it they also have to obey the law, I know, I know, Papa. We on the top must only claim we do. Those at bottom, the Nibelosers, they actually have to. That's why the *Riesen*, the giants, come in handy? Yes? Because the dwarfs are in constant quarrel with each other, you say? When could they have started to quarrel while having to work incessantly? That they can never come to an agreement and you don't have to pay your debts? That their union reps have long been in the nuthouse? They took their favourite party right along with them, right! You, wanderer, wounder of the law? Well, what's up? You'll have plenty to wonder about, all the things they will come up with, they'll brag about their forging skills for sure, forging is something you can't do, only they can do that. There are so many sorts of dwarfs and they all hate each other and even small improvements in their metal processing craft – everything they are specialized in, everything for which they have tools which demand a special skill and steady hand at forging – come to nothing if they are taken away from the easily agitated and hard to restrain master craftsman to entrust all that to a special mechanism, let's say: a machine. So finely constructed, but it hardly accomplishes anything fine, except maybe for the housewife's sewing. Competition among the skilled workers, dwarfs as well, but somewhat bigger, you bet. And thus they specialize more and more and earn less and less. Must resort to magic hoods, rings weighing a tonne, breaking their fingers and other nonsense, must protect their hands, prone as they are to all kinds of irregularities, with all kinds of absurd arrangements, should they no longer function and thus have to be replaced by machines which, of course, make no mistakes, but break easily. Then what? Repair dwarfs? Meanwhile those processes have been so well mechanized that a child can execute them. Even Siegfried, who really is a technical idiot, can do it, but he doesn't have to be able to do it. He works with *spukhafter Fernwirkung*, spooky remote effect, you only see the effect and are spooked. He went forth to learn what fear was, but never was spooked. All the dwarfs', all your efforts will be for the birds. While his machine does its work, he talks with the birds or lets his cock do the talking, pardon my English. But what do you call someone, who doesn't even know whom he fucks? Well, I know what I call him. And you are up to your neck in debts, Papa. You need gigantic sums for the giants. According to Adam Riese, that proverbial German math-giant, you can never pay them off. The machine replaces a number of adult hires with an even bigger number in dire straits, who now have nothing to do any more. They are not even the *Ersatzheer*, the Replacement Army, the relief army, they only recoil in horror that now they are nothing, have nothing and do not count at all. Trained craftsmen, and were they on hand only in the shape of dwarfs, or totally unhandy as giants, whose other end you can't even see in the fog, if you look at them from the bottom up which, by the way is just like in our new house, in the fog you can no longer see its roof from the ground, in *Nebelheim*, the fog home, what good is a house, if you can never see it as a whole?, especially if the others don't see it and envy us? – anyway, giants, dwarfs, machines, water, fog, rain, forest, animals, all these creatures get replaced by untrained jobbers at machines, which can't even sing like a little woodbird. They can't do anything, those machines. Yet people get replaced, even if there is nothing that could replace them, one by another, many by all, all by a few, the trained by the untrained and back again, from the unskilled to the skilled, as needed, none of them thinking, but someone guiding them. Telling them what to do. Many kept busy, but one does the bossing. Yes, Papa, I know, you don't. You have more debts than there are hairs on your head. You want to bag what your humankind-machinery produced. You don't want to pay your debts, and then you say, others are at fault. Not you. Always others. You make debts but punish others for their most grievous default. You do what you want. You want to pocket the profit of everything after the ones have been replaced by the others, men by women,

women by men, children by devices, through which their voices resound, whatever, in any case until no one knows any more where he belongs but doesn't worry about it, because he'll be told anyway. And you think that no one will know to whom you owe what! The gigantic pile of money, the ring, the sister-in-law, the profit from the apple plantation, whatever! The storm march you owe humankind so that it doesn't have to do it! Donner will produce the thunder for it and Froh the jolly good time. But no one talks about what jerks they are. However, something like the debt, the guilt, the *Schuld* one has cannot be easily packed in a suitcase and carried off like the money one needs to square it up. One never comes square with anything and neither with one-self. Absurd agreements, even contradicting each other, who can figure it all out! I see lawyers! I see three women coming beneath the earth, I could have done with one, I would have immediately left the construction work in a way that it would rain in – oh no, not those three – yes, exactly, those with their crochet work, and what will come of it? Not even a scarf, not even a potholder! They murmur darkly, goaded, of course, by their mama, the good Earth, I visited her too, no idea what her problem is, always in a huff, just for the heck of it, and I still visit the Earth, her daughters in the background, they carry their detail tools in their throats and put them to use. They can hang themselves on their yarn for all I care. I don't give a damn about whatever they say. I used to have this sword, it must still be somewhere, I'd gladly cut their rope right through with it and then them too, I'd hack through all of them, makes no difference any more. I've already done everything else. Others do more, but does it do them any good? The worker is there, but the worker will be unsellable, his product, however, anyone can have. So why contracts? Let me answer for you: because you don't have to honour them. You could have really said that sooner. It isn't so complicated. The work is there, but the worker becomes unsellable like paper money taken out of circulation, and your contracts become invalid, Papa, just because you want it that way. There is no one left above you, at your command fires burn, giants toil, dwarfs smash in each other's faces. But this won't end well, Papa. All of us know that the loan which, by the way, never was paid out, but rather only promised, you will never be able to pay off. You will have to let your wealthy friends help you. Lower interest rates. But throwing such a left hook and risking such a thick lip, Papa, I never thought you would do that. That you'd get into the credit crunch just because you got involved with the wrong guys and in the meantime can't even tell who they actually are. Doesn't matter, you don't intend to pay and you can't be confronted as a debtor, as you must always wander, you are travelling, gone fishing, first you built the house and now you are never there. Besides, the right ones don't interest you anyway. Don't talk nonsense! Whoever deserves something, doesn't get it. The one who is to wed the bride doesn't get her either, even though he is entitled to. Light elves, black elves, shadow elves, Dobby, those dwarfs come in more races than dogs! And you owe all of them, money or something else or *Schuld*, yes, guilt itself! I can only congratulate you, Papa. You did it, owing everyone, even yourself and still no sense of *Schuld*. You simply have no feel for debt! You might still be downgraded, I just don't know by whom! The grade would be far too steep for anyone, well, maybe not for you, you'll flat out deny the grade and by a hair you'll make the grade. Where you are not, there's nothing but death.

And where you are ditto. Plenty of death for all of us at the end, or it wouldn't be called the end. You are the dream, the comfort and the hope of all sufferers, but once I am asleep behind your fire not even you'd manage to come through to me, it won't matter to me any more. If you weren't our President, you couldn't indulge in any of this. If you weren't God, you could at least walk through a fire you didn't start yourself. Now a sea of embittered helplessness, acquired recklessness. You always believed – back when you commissioned the construction of this monumental one-family home in that dump, the name of which I have forgotten – a name one would think can't really be for real, Mr President, only when all of this will go under, will I remember again – so you believed that you can do whatever you please, Papa, just because you are God, a destroyer tearing down the law he made himself! I had not considered that you would kill all the people you owe, at least ensure it will be done, death, after all, is the only thing you always make sure of. Not a bad method, except that it will end some time when no one will be left. The supply of workers is inexhaustible, at least it seems so because we don't see any any more, the unskilled don't die out, there are just two pieces of giants. They are rare. Soon only one, though he will be broken too, by the hero, no, by himself, by the other giant, herewith we declare the line extinct, broken, for once not by the law. You can handle them, they are already weakened anyway! Been given the count. You didn't pay out. It won't pay off for us. Just take a look how they are crawling around like worms, hauling, piling, mortaring, water logging, waterlooing. And you'll surely find some sucker for any home improvement work! It's always like that. The president in his office: one singular mafia! The god at his walking staff: one singular absurdity. So he's got his new house and for what? His own will as master of man, his lust his only law? Ridiculous! His own power his only property? Well, we've seen where that leads to. Nations, listen, listen for once!, so, okay, they've heard it already, so what? I finally can go to sleep. No wonder you don't want to go home, Papa, to the newly constructed home you own! And you will own up to it, no question. If man, *der Mensch*, gets destroyed together with his active, creating power, his *schaffende Kraft*, good God, I am actually writing this down!, but if I just say it you don't listen to me, Papa, so then, if the *Mensch* gets destroyed, he must first smash the violence of his owners. He absolutely must do that, don't forget! But this is something only the giants can do. And only one of those is left. You, however, a god, whom should you smash? What good would it do? Well, you'll do it to me, I can see it coming. And a man, a hero of course, we don't do it below that, this man is to get me, a free man, a saint, then bring your shit to the station or deposit it right on the loo-and-behold-spot, Papa, a Saviour! Come to me, move it now!, our salvation work is already in process, but man's work is and remains lifeless. You can destroy his order, take everything away from him, spur him on to anything, but death will come, to the slave as to the master all the same, equal in death, but not in terms of who was who, fundamentally unequal is what they are, he comes for me and the lord and master, the saviour who knows no fear, even though he'd like to get to know it, he is very sociable, the more the merrier: he who will come, oh, I don't know either, and then death will come. All this for what? I don't even know what for. I don't know either, is it any wonder? The Saviour, the Redeemer will know: where and what he will be able to redeem. And that's no wonder. There are no miracles. Oh, and the coup of employing giants because they don't need machines, I don't know if that was smart. At the moment, certainly, but then? Machines quiet down at some point, humans never. The dwarfs, of course, were pissed off, because they did not meet the requirements, you know which ones, and because whatever they forged was always taken away from them. How they'd have loved to keep it, but it's not the purpose of labour, doing it all for oneself only. Then nothing would get done! Poor munchkins! You would have had to put a hundred of them on top of each other to mortar a single stone. No, that wouldn't have worked, though you could have also invested in ladders or fire engines, they are listed on the stock market and not badly at all. Grand-scale gold-smithing much smarter. Gold's always needed. Hold it, how is it doing right now, well it dropped some, but still bullish. No shit! You bet. Gold trumps. You know what? We simply kidnap it! But that's not so simple, so let others do it, as usual. They all were pure and guiltless, at least that's what they claim, before the gold was forged. What everyone needed, they got, what harms the other is what they are doing now. Slaying each other, the giants are not the first in that, they stand on a pile of slain bodies, though they really wouldn't have to make themselves bigger than they are. They should make gold, if stealing is so dangerous, it weighs on the conscience, with which you can't pay for your one-family home either, Papa! Who'll buy something for your conscience, Papa! And from that spear, where you foolishly wrote down everything – I've been telling you again and again, never anything in writing! – no one could copy anything from it if he's planning a decent fraud. To each his own crime! Rich auntie Freya whose estate no one will inherit because she'll never die, you can bank on that, she might pay. Would be unwise to kill her, as she can't die, but it would be generally unwise to let her go, since you would thus forego your most important capital and need cosmetic surgery to gloss over your age, you made-up corpses! What goes out, must also come in again. Youth goes away, old age is coming. Freya is free again and joins Thor in the Land of the Freer and the wrinkles creep back up on all of you again. Whatever. You don't have to pay anyway and you won't pay. The dwarfs produce the money and more meanies, I mean peewees, holding it for them. Until it gets taken from them, like everything. You beget heroes, so what! You exhale so much breath from your chest, the heroes couldn't even inhale all of it! Beautiful stuff, jewels, rare pieces among them, no argument there. This ring alone! Yes. This ring alone. One of a kind. But they won't be allowed to keep it, even though they deserve it, those wretched Alberichies. What worker would have ever been allowed to keep what he earned. They learned quickly, the alps, no, the *Alben*, those elves, the dwarfs, they bunched up, in the *Alben*-album they were bunched up like alpinists' photos of radiant heights, which would have been okay, but then they instantly battered each other again. Forged swords, which kept falling apart, mechanically, they might not have been quite up to speed, the others, however, were even worse. Not even you, Papa, paid close enough attention when you learned how to forge. You did not master the craft. Others had to do it. A god doesn't have to learn anything, he is and that's enough. For him, at least. The rest of them: everyone against everyone! Always! Instead of being united against you. They sensed that only one will get it right with the sword and that one, unfortunately, will be an idiot. And where

will he end up? With me, of course, typical! I am the
dumping ground for heroes. Having one dwarf even just
toppling over for this one – which wouldn't make much
difference to the dwarf, he is very short anyway – not
necessary! Doesn't pay. He'll off that dwarf. As if that
were a feat. And you don't pay either. Your luck, Papa,
that they are always at each other's throats or don't even
yet exist, because you first have to produce them! They
always took something from someone, which in turn
will be taken from the new owners and so on and so on:
theft at the start, theft at the end, in-between deceit.
Property – theft. An endless chain of expropriation, just
so we can get our new house. I couldn't care less! I prefer
being at home in nature. Be in the stable with my horse,
like all girls. I don't care how you'll cough up the pay-
ments for the house, Papa, you cough and you cough,
lots of mucus, lots of slime, though all that ails you is a
missing eye, which now shines in the sky, where you really can't use it. No need for more injuries to a god who'd
rather be ingested or get consumed by flames. No, the
other eye does not tell anything either. No, sadly, it does
not speak to me. It just looks. I don't see what you gave it
away for, the eye, by the well, gave it away no, not for a
decision, for a forgiveness of debts, a forgiving of deeds
against all the dead, you wouldn't even dream of it, at the
well outside the gate, *am Brunnen vor dem Tore*, an eye for
nothing, nothing at all; I cannot call your decisions wise.
Your ravens don't even bother to comment. I don't blame
them. No, the wolves don't either, they have no part in
this. Instead, Fricka talks, non-stop. Her ramblings seg-
ue into shrill shrieking. A strong woman, as is so often
required now. Do you have to constantly cheat on her?
You once were so hot for her, you sacrificed your eye!
Now everyone's got hell on earth instead of the new

home. Was that necessary? Submit to the wayward sub-terrenean brood, which doesn't know breeding and subordination, no, not even they! Do you really have to put up with this? You are the President after all, or whatever you want to call it. Or a few floors above that, whatever, you can't be seen in the fog anyway, way up there, you with the magic wand for the law; it doesn't mean though that you have to wander constantly and thus drive your wife up the wall! The gods were always shapeshifters, no one keeps their shape, though that goes only for old age, but you gods have always been others and become others for those who wanted to adore you. Or call you to account, except: you always could count better than anyone else. Couldn't you have stayed yourselves, so that the blue-eyed, the believers, but not the creditors find you? Better get her a ring, you know which one! In whose face do you throw guilt like hay to an animal? Dominating the world, but not even able to forge a proper ring, you can really be proud of that, Papa! A ring, it's so simple. You take a piece of gold, make a hole in it and done. Then you throw it into the water, so that it gets value added, with little effort and then you get it out of there again with great effort or, rather, you let some sucker do it for you and then you do him in. Just so you can give it away again, the ring. Anyway, you could easily just command what's useful to you, end of story. Why pay at all? What do you care whether the worth of your new one-family home was created by the process of its construction, by its beautiful location on the mountain or by magic? Not even Marx thought of magic and he thought of everything. All the stuff that flowed into this house you absolutely had to have. The productive labour of two idiot giants flowed into it like the Rhine, with this gigantic substructure, which can't be seen in the river, age-old stuff, partly liquid, liquefied, partly a river filled with stuff, gold bulk trash, which does not increase the value of your property, because you remained indebted to the builders of this gold stuff? I don't know what's up any more. I think you will have to fork it out, thank *you*,[1] *you* don't either, up *yours* too, I talk and talk, thank *you* for the applause, I make no sense, thanks for the applause now rising like the Rhine every year at high water, thank *you*, well, what did I want to say, all those dwarf smithies' flailing little arms, the giants' mega-heavyweight labour steps, all the dead heroes we must drag around so that you can get your fresh cell therapy, Papa, and the heroes too, of course, there is always money for the military, all this is like the transmigration of creatures, whom you put into service. The work of all those beings, whether golden forms, solid, dripping, fluid or superfluous, whatever, the work of all these entities in their gigantic numbers and the giants in their rather small number, only two pieces, soon enough only one, what did I want to say, so all that productive labour of those ghostly labour-beings, no matter in what shape and size they appear, who manufactured your new product, your one-family house, all these constituent elements for the construction of the house of a god or president or whatever, this labour, all that labour benefits only you and your co-gods, actually fake gods, since there isn't much talk about them; so now, all of this, all of them go into – let's go now! – a transmigration of souls, which I mentioned earlier. The transmigration is on, it is not

1 'you' italicized indicates the capitalized, formal German address 'Sie' for you. In the text it is used to address the reader or audience as distinguished from the informal 'du' (you) between Brünnhilde and Wotan.

cancelled as was erroneously announced, on the contrary, it is on continuously, *you* can go in or out any time, you'll still get it all. The exchange value wanders in, it wanders out, it wanders in, it wanders out. In, out, in, out, it depends, but on what exactly I can't tell. Makes my tongue slip. I might put my foot in my mouth. I should say: I don't know, but I'll say a lot more, even though I am pretty clueless, which doesn't exactly increase my use value, but my exchange value: oho! Not bad! I made good use of the development of my social productive force, even though people helped me with that. So, should I keep saying things, I am not saying anything, so I go on saying something. Whatever. And the value of all these elements, of that whole brood which, by the way you haven't paid yet either, because it's supposed to pay off itself by the owners killing one another; thus, one owes less and less. What is the value, how does the exchange happen, how does it proceed, may I proceed: value, still waiting for it, for what it is, well, all this is based on first acquiring the other's commodity by selling one's own and the legal relationship in this is the contract, people, the legal persons exist for each other solely as representatives of commodity and thus as owners of commodity, they exist (and then they die off together with the State and together with it they go into the family grave, even though the State never behaved like a family towards them, well, maybe like mine towards me), until the commodity is gone or only until only one has something, but it won't be you, let me tell you, Papa, God!, I can tell you exactly what will happen to the house, first of all you will have to resign, no, you won't, yes, you will, at the time I am writing this it is not yet clear, ah yes, it is, resigned, just now!, I as an opportunist will use the outcome later, when it's delivered to me, all done, what did I want to say while I've been saying so much already, well, what?: so then, the still unpaid value, the payment of which you will continue to dodge, Papa this consumed, contorted body of a value which was created by the unappreciated, uncompensated, you think that as a god you can get away with everything, Papa, so this dis/contorted body of a newly created value in the form of a house – yes, newspapers, don't hesitate in writing this, I don't care, media, devices, trumpet it!, I only read postings that can teach people to think; makes no difference, even though I am related to you and it falls back on me – Papa, so this value, this consumed value which transformed into labour, no, the other way around, the contorted labour that became a value which, however, isn't a real value at all, not for us at any rate who are meant to pay for it, enters the newly created body of the product, the new house which we are also supposed to pay for and which you avoid, more or less since it stands. And with it the wife. You are nuts, Papa! So while the giants produced a value, their form of house construction, their forum for complaints and miscellaneous claims, in a book no one has to open, because it always is, for all (one of the God's question: which book doesn't ever have to be opened?), everything in it?, yes, their labour anyway, and the real work done noiselessly, furtively, secretly behind their backs, the actual work, that counts!, and that is called: appropriation, theft. Breach of contracts. That is the actual work, the non-payment, the draining, the taking away, the not-upholding of something that could not even be held if it were light as a feather, which would have to be caught first!, so, that's the real labour, the appropriate output, the expropriation of those who do it, that's the actual work and this is what you – when the labourer can't sell his labour power, because no one needs it any more – this is what you took over, Papa, as one who takes the labour power of, yes, even the intellectually challenged, but instead physically unchallenged power athletes in their weight rooms, from where they should have never been taken, so then you are the one who takes the man-power and does not change it into value added, but adds more value! More added value than the value added, which is always produced anyway. That's normal. This house, by never having been paid for, is absolutely unsellable, because it has no value. No, all wrong. Labour was added by the giants, payment was promised, but in the end: nada. In the end nothing. Only the product stands, it has no more traits of labour, that's all we'd need. Those contorted traits no, trains, well, both, with which those commuters travel to work, every workday, over and over again, delayed trains, running around, rushing, the child still has to be dropped off at kindergarten, the husband still has to be railed at and the train isn't coming, just looking at all those trains, those traits, that's too much for anybody. Those are not the traits of a god. This solid fortress does not show the traits of a god. This mighty fortress is not our god. The mighty fortress belongs to our god, though in principle it's the same and it is more than if he were it, the fortress. Enormous amounts of money get moved, but not paid out. Absolutely nothing gets paid. The money is here, it lives, it does not work, okay, it did before, now it no longer works, it simply is around, it's always someone else who's got it, for what, the money, gold, it glitters, I know, Papa, you want to have your cake and eat it too and you actually can do it, you greedy guy!, glutton god, good greed!, so help us gods, if it makes you vomit, help yourself, help yourself to anything you want, for others pay, or rather no: others won't get paid to begin with. Dwarfish brood, giant brutes, I mean prudes by default thus unable to find a woman, small wonder, considering their bodies' build – fortunately they gave our building a reasonable body! – such a woman would be standing on a ladder all the time, like the dwarfs at work, all of them having to elevate themselves by necessity and if it takes stepping on others, since stepping over them would take too long, what did I want to say, I always want to say something, but no one listens, you are gone anyway and have been for quite some time, like most papas, I don't see you, you the half-sighted, blindsiding deal-breaker. I don't really mean any of this, you hear me, it is a gift of nature, the labourer's natural gift others don't have, he's got it, a gift that costs him nothing, no wonder he gifts it, but it brings in a lot for the owner, the owner of humans, the God. But no, sorry, that was earlier. I always go backwards when I actually want to get ahead. We have been further ahead but keep going back. That whole house, for what, Papa? What's it all about? Just so you finally won't stray any more, says Fricka. But you could have lived in the gold! You wouldn't have needed the house, you could have lived right in the *Schatz*, the treasure, the *Hort*, the hoard, the playground of the children of the Rhine! Maybe it was too noisy there for you. You rather go for the mothers, who are ready for pick-up, ready for anything, for anyone who picks and gets them out of there. And then the constant pounding and banging and all this by the batty to boot. Why that stupid house, since you won't pay for it anyway and that entire *Schatz*, well, well, well!, is still here. Okay, yes, here it is, but you haven't got it! You don't pay, you owe – so, owing to this or not owing to this, in any case, no one owes you, you don't own it either. So, you didn't even want to pay. You turned it on its head and – sorry for hitting you over the head with this, Papa – you wouldn't have needed that fucking fortress, if you did not want to pay for it. We should only use what we can pay for. Using that house is no pleasure, it is the exchange value that yields all the pleasure. That no one else can have it, the house. But where does that leave the exchange value? It grasps at nothing. How can the accumulation of goods be an incentive, if only we own and use these goods? Besides, no one pays for nothing but everyone always pays for it. No pay, but everyone pays for it. All of you were guile- and guiltless, sure, before money existed, before gold was forged. What someone needed was given to him by another. But what's harming the other is what they do now that they are sitting on their money. They are killing each other! Papa, I almost think the gold would have been better protected by you, no kidding. Had you paid with it for the house right off, order could have kicked in, which you, in turn, could have kicked in again like a pressboard door, but afterwards. Now everyone is doomed to die, yes, you too and so am I, so are all of us. If you don't pay for the house, but even if you do, it doesn't matter, it is doomed to decay or it isn't, no, not yet, but I think it, our house will fall, because you won't have paid for anything. Or too late, too little, paid with the wrong currency, or paid the right one to the wrong party?, you might even have wanted to pay, but others got the better of you, just promise them everything, you don't have to give it to them!, yes, I know, at least you wanted to, while others manage will-lessly. All that brouhaha, but no payment; tricks get concocted, coercive laws invented (dear giants, at least have some understanding, even though you have no brains, we are much worse off than you!), excuses cooked up, ears talked off, innards traded, stockpiles invaded and meanwhile the capital is expanding, the fortress expands, even though the gods haven't multiplied in a long time, everything expands just to be maintained, everything expands, it grows into the Nothing, because whatever exists is completely filled but what grows most gladly, most quickly, the mostest, is capital if treated correctly, if homeownership-fever can be stoked, if the regulations for creditors – those weird creatures, giants and dwarfs, between them normal ones, who, though, don't want to follow any norms – become ever more permeable, ever more pliable, ever more unreliable, if financial institutions introduce teaser rates on the market, if one has hardly any or no capital at all, but absolutely wants a house, you've got to live somewhere, don't you, no capital, it doesn't grow like the golden apples, thus it has to work very hard to grow, but ultimately everything keeps growing, like real estate prices before, not any more now, not before, now they do, prices which also always keep growing and growing, faster than the golden-delicious apple saplings, that's how it goes. Everything flows, everything grows and that which grows also falls again, it drops, but, ultimately, it's always growing, only the real estate, poor thing, goes under, because there is no more cash flow to water it. Up to now they always kept growing and will continue to do so. But if you actually are going to pay, Papa, pay with the gold you stole, property is theft and, in the end, there are only thieves, so then, if you pay, others fall. All fall because of money. Money fells them all. If you'd lived right in the money from the start, no fortress could have been burnt, I wouldn't have had to burn up either, nor my poor horse, who's got nothing do with it, no, nobody would have had to get burned if you had ponied up all right, you did, but it was never enough. In the end you always kept more than you spent. Others were wasted, completely spent. You only had expenditures. No one could harm you, no one could have harmed you, if you – you and your fellow gods – wouldn't have been already prepared for disaster and susceptible to it. The dwarf with his ring wouldn't have hurt you. Some manual work wouldn't have hurt you either. The wilful wants of humans are like money, the Norns' golden wool is also like money. Everything is like money, because it is money, anything that counts and can be counted. All that effort and for what? For that! The love between you and your wife, the strong tie that ties everything, which you always untie so easily, Papa, it makes each of you the warrantor of the other, I don't know another word, I only know the warranty obligation with regard to other things, to capital, that is, securing it, insuring it, yes, also the capital of your love, this ongoing insuring, double, triple insurances between the two of you, beyond the necessary changes of love, for which no one would issue a bill of exchange, this counteracting everything that must constantly renew itself, that should change, sink into the ground and wake up and grow again as a plant, the changeful in general, when the bills of exchange have already been issued and all of us are exposed like puppies, blind, deaf, toddling and whimpering, this countering of change gets the bill of exchange to expire even faster, to exit the date that's written on it and run away, guaranteeing its owner everything, turning it all to stone like your single-family house, Papa, and what turns into the hardest stone are those joined together heretofore, you and your wife and the two of you swing that which never happens, you swing the standstill, which might just stand still for the sake of the interest, not for me, as for me it doesn't have to, it stands still, it has to, it could run off, after all, it's for the interest and compound interest, the standstill's just standing there, even though it would rather take a hike, wander, like you, Papa, be on the move, move through the interest and compound interest, no idea where to, but now standstill and that is also where it's at with your spousal love and the pain of lovelessness and lifelessness begins. Because securedness is standstill. Yes, Papa, everything shuts down when love is on lockdown. You wander, by yourself. You, the plan-maker who makes no plans and does not stick to them! You aren't even a capitalist, don't need to, those down there are, if they can swing it not having to sweat any more; you don't even want to bag value added any more, want nothing, give nothing, you are nothing, Papa, a god, after all, doesn't have to be something, true enough, HE IS, as long as you can rake it all in and hand out nothing, there are no rules for you, you don't see the free gift of labour, such as: the dwarfs' longing, who can't even think of something like that, as that of the giants' for a woman, a woman, for a woman as I am one. For example. As if a woman were worth money, as if a woman had ever been worth the money, not hers of course, very rarely hers, no, the other's money, of course, a woman's always worth some kind of currency, but her currency does not last long, her youth, that is, when a woman is still worth something. Well, but her apples you should keep, otherwise not even that woman would be worth anything among you guys. Only in her youth does she have value and that can be paid for if so desired. Freya breeds the apples and with them pays herself. Thus she is freer than her *Freier*, okay, sorry, sorry, sorry, boo, boo, boo! I heard you, so now you can stop again. Woman is the rottenest and the quickest to

28

spoil. I, supposedly the object of someone's desire?, one who apparently can't count, isn't that grotesque?! They've got the *Schatz*, they work for you gratis, you take the hoard, you take it from them again, never mind what's engraved in that stupid ash shaft of your weapon, but what do they all want? A woman's all they all want. That's their lowest common denominator. A woman. They plan and they sweat and then they want nothing but a woman. Well, not all of them, however, if not, there's *zoff*, for our foreign born fellow citizens there'll be crumbs, they'll crush each other underfoot, they don't need their own parade for that, the fighters, they follow anyway and don't even know whom they're following; it's like at a love parade with too many participants for so little love. They also want gold, the giants, who could crush all of them at once if they wanted to, but if they can't have that, they want a woman. Fifty-fifty. One the woman, the other the money. That would be ground zero, even ground forces could be deployed, had we not spent everything already for the house. Well, okay: if a woman, if that's what it has to be, then one who sits on golden apples! Who lays golden eggs? That's the least one can ask for. They want to become serfs for the money or they want to become serfs for the woman. The woman, however, decides nothing, she does not decide, because you decided for her already. A wanderer as shameless panderer against the law!, it's all good, throw them the ring, it won't change a thing, everyone's used to your spontaneous actions and eruptions, Papa. What follows are ruptures and rapes and retribution, perjury and adultery, on and on endlessly, everyone punished, everything punished, swiftly committed, swiftly corrected. Law and order: the guardians of the oaths are the biggest lawbreakers. You know what I mean, Papa. The guilty don't pay their debts. They avenge them constantly, but to pay them is out of the question. They are disloyal, but they pay for loyalty, they want the golden apples for payment of the house and at the same time they want to keep them like their youth! And it works! They bring order, yes, of course that's what they call disorder, that's the one they bring, as everyone knows. That is what they want. What everyone wants is all they know. I know that you see it differently. Can you please tell me, Papa, what I want? For I don't know myself. A woman for the giants, okay, here we go, there she is, we've got the carnal part, now we just need one for the carnage, or something we can put into it, the way the labourer puts his life into his labour to produce surplus value for the capitalist. That's how it used to be, that's how it used to be, now it's all gone, now it doesn't exist any more. Now it doesn't work any more. The worker wants to, but who'd still want him? The money stays. It doesn't work any more, it simply becomes more and more, I already said it many times and yet, it is true, it's making the rounds, it haunts the world, contracts mean nothing to it, it doesn't even read them, that reckless money, nothing can happen to it anyway!, what should happen to it!, it makes the rounds, from one to another, it becomes more, no one knows how, no one knows why, there is so much of it and yet, you won't pay for your house or too late or too little, that's how it always is, Papa, there will always be too little, especially for a god, he is priceless, especially when he cracks jokes and tears down houses, which are already crumbling, well, that's how it is: even though there is so much money, just lying around, doing nothing, not even earning interest, without interest even in your special interests, people go on as if nothing happened. Yes, there they go, they'd gone on killing sprees, but now they just went for a walk. A short walk around the block. No one has seen them. They want to kill and also kill themselves, first the former then the latter, but absolutely not vice versa!, no, we didn't know them. Unknown hereabouts, we never saw them going by, but it certainly couldn't have been the Holy Trinity, because one person was a woman! Who is it taking a walk there, it can't be the three, we've never seen them, taking a walk, fine, but only round the corner, money doesn't get taken out like people, that's a no-go, money goes on its own, but one must watch it, at least come up somehow with the interest, or it is gone, else the house is gone, this time not blown up, just gone, well not just, it's just that someone else has it, no one has it, it hasn't been paid for and now it belongs to the bank and gets lost, because everything gets lost that's entrusted to the bank, even words get lost in the bank or they are denied. But I told you that I sold you this high risk product, I didn't tell you?, it doesn't matter, the main thing is I knew it, yes, the money is running out now, it has to get to a safe place, it's the last thing that can still escape. It's always too little anyway. That's what it comes down to, it is always too little. There is always too little in the packets or the wrong thing. And what do they want, what do they want, what did those, who at least had money in their fingers through which it keeps running, want to have? And why? Why didn't they want money to be abolished altogether? Those who have nothing are all for it and they are the majority. Money, after all, has become nothing but information, where to get it and what to do with it, it disappeared underneath it, so let's get rid of it for good! Now you can hardly see it any more, anywhere, like those two men and that woman, they weren't seen anywhere, though they were residents and malcontents in Zwickau. Active folks, on the go as goons, the stallions were joined by a mare and enjoyed grazing together. Believed to be unarmed, gutless goofs, on the contrary: heroes, German heroes do the killing themselves, they don't leave it to anyone else. Too much fun. Let their cutting-edge savour that foreign brood, which we can surely brutalize with weapons. Who? Who are *you* talking about? Who were they supposed to be and where? Never seen them. Never heard of them. Money: thank you very much, but I haven't seen it in a long time. Can't tell you where it is or who's got it. I? Certainly not! It disappeared in the fog, it can't represent an independent value, because the value can no longer be seen by anyone. The value has been outsourced, it is made of air, but not everybody breathes the same air. One can breathe abroad and so the money happens to be there. It's gone, to more beautiful places, wherever, just gone. Never saw it. We don't know it. This here used to be our club house, but what's in there now – no idea. There is no money in it for sure, we would know about it. It was once produced as debt, not a nice thought, God knows, but what is it doing now other than fill us with dread? Who wants it, who doesn't yet have it? Who wants nothing? Who does not have nothing yet? Still someone who's still got some? Junk can be discontinued, since those who still want it can replace it, cashless happiness! But that's not going to work. No way! Only the money keeps going, always away from us. Only we will go, be gone forever, sometime. Those two men whom no one saw, no one knew, *nie sollst du mich befragen*, never shall you ask me, they also were gone. Gone for broke. Pulled out of their house's family's tree, the only one that grows here and their bullets sure licked them all, those bullets kept licking around, like it?, yes, we do like that fiery thrust. Shot dead in the end and blown to pieces. It was fun with the foreigners, but we also did it to ourselves. Tat for tit. Done to me as done to you. Same difference, get them, those foreigners. Trust the weapon! They also work wonders with us. We are gone, the gods, however, will not go and they won't fly either, you will, Papa, but not they, they won't go like us, they won't collect air miles and become gold-card-bearing senators, they are gods already after all, they won't go, those high up, the highest-up colleagues, but we will. The gods with their honest needs for More will stay and bunker it, as they themselves are programmed for eternity. Well, gotta first have it! But the golden apples are just as good, even though the money is no longer hitched to gold, each goes its own way, it takes more and more money to pay for gold, it might not pay off to have so much gold. The gods, yes, exactly, I mean those who have lived in their houses, will be no more eternal than money, than guilt, than debts, than interest, no, wrong, only interest will be the eternal, why else would money exist if not for becoming more, ever more? Forever more. And eternity expands like the universe. And then the More even more! They will spend it on a house, the gods, that's the money that doesn't belong to them. Everyone, after all, spends the money that doesn't belong to them. Everyone lives their debt-ridden guilt and must constantly create money as if out of water in order to pay for it. The giants, the dwarfs, Mime, Alberich, all the same, what do they want, much work time would be gained if they'd finally announce that we must renounce everything. That's what they want, so they should also tell us. They want that which lies around masterless everywhere, no, that, whose master many claim to be, whatever there is, wandering around, all by itself, moved also by giant hands no one can see, not even a god, the money is there, the money is here now, look at the indicator board!, the money just arrived. The proof is shown on the board in blazing letters. Don't *you* want to pick it up? It's just waiting for it. *You* want to spend it and keep it, everyone wants that: just as the gods avenge guilt and at the same time want to become guilty, consecrate everything only to desecrate it again. What do the gods really want? Look it up! What does the good Earth say to it? What does Earth talk about at the donor conference she convened herself? The Earth gives, but what does she say, what justifications will she give when one day she won't give any more? What the gods do NOT want they must want, but they never want what they don't want and therefore they must perish some day. The Earth sees her end before her. She sees the money lying around as if it were nature, the money is in the hoard, waiting to board and sail offshore. Until then human muscles push the money into the concentration of production plants. But those will also fall. The gods will fall, but it won't fall into our hands, it will belong to those who have no right to it, because they take their right out of their own hands. That is injustice. I, at least, think so. There, look, right there a brother already clobbers his brother, killing him. He doesn't listen, he doesn't look out, yet he is what he is only through treaties and contracts, but he doesn't believe it. He doesn't want to hear it. No one wants to hear it, not even a god. Who'd want to hear something like that? Honouring treaties, you must be kidding!, rejecting the especially favourable loan interest rates, just because you are a god? No way, José! The gods decisions are a joke, why should they reimburse for something humans wouldn't know what to do with, why should they trade a goddess for money, when the idiots, the builders, those body buildings, the giants wouldn't know then what to do with her? Well, one does, he raves about her shining eyes. But the money shines easily ever more brightly. Deception is so easy! The bargain home-loan – so easily swiped! The wife, so easily acquired and abandoned again! The money. Not even acquired. The treasure, not honestly acquired. By whom, by the way? Secured by contracts, which they are not, because nobody abides by them. The gold, the *Geld*, the money, simply there, end of story. No, simple it is not. I say this all the time. What do *you* want, what could *you* possibly still want, when the money is always there, but always figures – aplenty – some other place, though if you reach for it, it's always gone, some other place, bingo!, where it participates in the free wastage of humans. You!, who rule through beauty, glittering glorious sex, always still shining brighter than you is the money. No organ could ever keep up with it, not even the biggest, and that is man himself. A pitiful sex, really, but, mind you, he wants it that way. It loves to play along, the money, the gold, in strip mines, underground mines, any kind of goldmine. Fooling around, expressing itself in things. No more labour power behind it, that's long over, that's long past, that's all been done with long ago, everyone's working, but the money's always just there, so what's the catch? It always belongs to someone else. I don't get it, what could they want if the money's there already any-way? Why can't *you* be that other one, *you* have always been the other one, why not this time? Tell me, how's gold doing right now? No, I am not interested in what gold is doing these days, but how it is doing right now. Howdy doody, Mr Moody? Pretty goody. Somewhat down, but it'll easily rebound, as long as there are people, I mean suckers, it always catches up, even if no one stands in line in front of it. The only value there is, only the other suckers don't believe it. The suckers are always half-half, they don't go halves, they are half-half and I know which half I go for. Not going badly, either, not doing badly at all, not as well as it did once, but still quite well. Still better than we are doing. The gold is owned, it is owed to be owned by someone. God, that's some sea-sawing market! One can hardly steady oneself on Earth, who is asleep, carefree and forever, no matter what we do. The building of the house is left to the giants, they are the best at it because they are so big. The rules for underground work don't hold for them, and as to their product, whatever!, what still holds?, does it still hold that the value factor of the manpower and thus the amount of the surplus value is worth more only, when the worker who produces it – Mime, Alberich, everyone listen! – can use it for his mobility? When he can finally, after fifteen years, buy himself a new car. But listen to me: the worker does not exist any more! We came to an agreement on this. We just did. That's the lowest common denominator for those who have nothing in common and are greedy enough to agree. Always. Now a bit more is written on the paycheque. Good. Who should stomach this so that a surplus value can be consumed and by whom? No one there. No one at home. The giants are building the house, but they aren't there. And then they kill each other. Okay, workers have always done it when they were ordered to and those at least did it only after the gods' fortress was finished, have you seen this house? Did you ever look at it? For gods incredibly cheapo. A single-family house for a god plus wife! Hard to believe that giants built this. And they all want a woman, at least all who produced something, yes, and the giants too, and what's in it for them? What's there for the asses who busted their asses? Nothing left. Nothing to be done. At least they don't kill each other, although it would be pretty practical right now, so that, for example, the pressure of the surplus population would not increase. One could use this pressure for something else, one could set something in motion. They just kill each other for the heck of it, the one giant the other, the other one also tries it, but he dies, because those two *Riesen* can't stand each other. That's a reason. Maybe there is also another. Ultimately, they always kill each other for money or a woman or both. Sweating, with blistered hands, to win a wife, win money, if a wife's not available, who'd call such purchase twisted? Hey, listen, *Riese*, the woman as is, even one with golden apples, doesn't count. It's much badder to take her away from the gods. That's how it goes. Nicer than having money is taking it from someone. But at least they are doing something, the giants. And they can put two and two together. Way to go! Given the distance between the hand and the brain! Not bad. They don't organize the collaboration between the employed and the unemployed. They build a house and then they kill each other or are taken out by a third force, no, no, they'd rather do it themselves. One falls by the wayside, the other is the plundered part of the way. They are not needed any more. They don't get paid anyway. Or one takes all and gets killed later. We can wait that long. The usufruct, you heard right, that's the right to enjoy the apples they don't get, their eternal use they don't get, the *Riesen*. They get nothing at all. They are superfluous, overflowing like the Rhine, because the flow could just as well be elsewhere. Wherever there is a bed, it lies down on it. Wherever there is room, it flows into it, the river. When it gets too big, it also can climb up stairs beyond the banks. Money, the money does all this by itself, it does it independently, the money doesn't need anyone any more, no people, no stores, no contracts, not even an owner. Silence. Nice and quiet. All quiet, finally. Now the money no longer needs a contract for it to do something. It's all fired up to make something out of itself and then people get burnt for it in turn. Now they don't need contracts any more. It doesn't matter. The money does nothing, it just wanders like a god with his staff. It wanders around the earth. No one has it, no one sees it. It's simply there, albeit not everywhere, of course. And the guardians of the treasure, what do they want, what on earth do they want? They are just the guardians, after all and have no claims. They all are full of claims, as everyone's got claims who files them. They want a woman. A woman is what they want. Should she be the one to watch the money? Makes sense to me. Would be even better if she could produce it. But in a division of labour this will also be divided. There is great fear but also desire. Money, not bad, eternal youth even better. So why then money at all? I want to do something, but at the same time I am afraid of it. I fled out of fear to grant to myself what my father had given to me. You, Father, gave it to me. And now you contemplate some other pay? Always money, always more money, where is it supposed to come from, Papa? We aren't shitting money, oh, okay, I am sorry, of course we've got Freya, she can do it. Still, I don't regret that I moved out. I've got my own work, which fulfills me completely. If the giants get their wages, for this awful house, where I would not want to live anyway, we are fucked. You often paid giants, so then pay this one too, pay this time too, Papa! Ingratitude isn't always the reward, but this time it is.

38

The child clasps your knee. Father! Don't trample the child, don't dash me to pieces! I did what I shouldn't have done, but I am still afraid. Always only afraid. Don't know myself why. Why did you give me that stupid spear if I wasn't supposed to use it? But I don't dare to anyway. And then my last boyfriend smashed it to boot. Freud would have had to say a few things to this, had he been asked. The sons shall not sit armed at the father's table, but the father should not brag about his staff so much that it challenges the sons. Why did you promise me a sword, Papa? Or at least someone who can hold it, who can make it, both, for a change. Why did you promise me a hero? Typical, you make promises and don't keep them! And so now I can't keep up: Something's flowing out here, what is it?, before it was ink that came out of my spear, now I type and type and type, endless sentences, endless pages, endless bits and bytes, endless, you can't see why, but: here it is!, so now I can't stop it! Help! Do *you* see any sign here that I have even the slightest intention to stop? Do *you* see this here ever coming to an end? Well, there *you* see!, what a senseless effort, I know, I know, Father, this wasn't your order. Doing this, doing that. Doing anything at all, besides carrying heroes, inside and outside. So then away I hurry, eastward bound. Dressed to kill. Not everyone sees me the way I see myself. Someone says, that woman's make-up was applied with a shotgun. That is so mean! That man must be blind! I worked so hard on myself! We keep running and running, we reach the rock where I must sleep, alone. Money at least is doing something. I, however, have to sleep. But I don't have to do anything, you tell me, you, who never pays for anything but still has everything. I can't stop, I cannot stop right here, it should be so easy to simply put my hands in my lap, pick up the hero, carry him around a bit, and that's the end of it. Stop it! Stop it! Thank you, folks! I am trying, honestly! I'd just have to stop the work and be quiet or do something else or go on holiday and do nothing. That's how senselessly tired I am. Wouldn't mind sleeping, but a fire just for that isn't necessary, really. Okay, okay, I am pulling myself together! Mustn't fall asleep, it would be all over then! Yes, I know, everyone wants me to stop and finally sleep, but I don't want to, can't just accept everyone yawning at my stupid whining, I want to laugh about hunger and thirst, water and rocks, want to show that I permit myself the luxury of judging, permit me: your judgement! You will hear it only from me. I want to keep going! It's burning everywhere? What do I care? It's been burning far too often! Let's stop the burning or we'll die of our failures, of our inner impossibilities, Father! Carrying heroes, always carrying, always carrying others, yes, that would have been better, albeit not for me. Dragging heroes around, so that they can get out of my arms into your army, instead of scribbling on and on here! My fingers are more diligent than the law of demand! But where there is nothing, everyone has lost the right. Who? What? I should take them in too? I am not your recruiting officer! These are supposed to be heroes, that limp loot? I wouldn't have taken them. They are dead already! What do you want to do with them? You want to recruit them? For some battle on some side? For the *Endkampf*, the grand finale? There are no more sides and no more battles. Only the end. Nonetheless, I'd still like to be part of it, wherever. Please, not the shame that all I do is sleep, like the whole *Volk*, understanding nothing, doing nothing any more! Not allowed to schlepp heroes around any more. At least that was better than nothing, even though they were not alive any more. Deeds rather than words! Doughnuts rather than murders! So then others must read that I may go on writing. Why else would I be doing it? But they must contribute something to it as well. Their spirit must quietly move along and then it once makes one move too many and the connection to my one and only dear reader is cut off. You'll think of something, Papa, to keep your daughter busy and also the heroes, in the rear. Never pressing my divine mouth onto another? That too? I can't even imagine doing nothing. Schlepped heroes, not wise was I, never thought manual work was right for me; the thing with writing, who would understand it, even though so many are doing it, everything chuck-full of them, still more stuff to read arrived just now, delivered by an army of Amazons in a package solution. What else is one to do when one is always at home? Behind the fire? No love, *Liebe*: *verboten*. But you, of course, you, Father, you may protect, but you don't do it. Don't even protect me any more. In battle I guarded your back, yes, that's right, covering your ass. Whatever is in front of me doesn't interest you, I am always behind you, Father, only one eye anyway, Father, with it you see everything in front, I, I see behind your back what you don't see. With my backlights I see it, no, just a moment, think!, it's your backlights that are behind! What I saw as light was simply your backside, which I always see, since you are always one step ahead of me, you grandstander for the unfree. To them you seem mighty, like the sun! Might you want to free me, or stamp on me, no, put a stamp on me, which adds value to the writing? Telling it how far it will get? I only see what you don't see, Papa. I am blind, deaf, stupid, but my hands are still stirring, they stir like the giants in their mortar, like the new heroes with their murders, like the brother with the

41

sister. Everything stirs, everything moves. Everyone does what they shouldn't do. Only the money does it selflessly, big deal, it doesn't have a self, for its owners, who are always different ones. The money wanders like you, Father. But it has both eyes open. It keeps both eyes open, even though it is so unfeeling and it doesn't care where it lands.

W: My, my – Child! You've never said that much. I've listened to you for hours now but what have you said? I don't know any more. You want a double wedding but don't know who the other two should be. Many girls wanted that and then there suddenly were three and they were superfluous! And everyone wants a hero, sure, whom else. One guile- and guiltless, who assumes the debts and continues to pay. I: an example, but not a good one! Who became master by way of contracts, am now the servant of the contracts. A *Mensch* must come, first a human being's got to get here, one as we have never seen, because those we know can't do it. Someone we can dump it on. Nothing will come from me any more, I had my opportunities, absolutely, but now a real *Mensch* must come, who can do it better. Someone I don't have to help, that would be a first. One who, a stranger to the god, lives free of his favour, unconsciously, I mean, without knowing that there is a god at all, whoever he may be, in this case me, doesn't matter, conscious, unconscious, without anyone pulling the strings, he would pull it all off, the deed, no matter which one. The deed. Which is preceded by multiple views and those have backlights too. Whenever the brakes are hit, additional ones light up, it's often very interesting in the back, often there is too much braking, at first the motion can be noticed only from the back. That's when one should run in the opposite direction or the motion must be fought. Without me. That's it. I would not have to advise him, not help him, not wish him anything. He wouldn't even know that I am the only one who may wish anything at all, this friendly foe, where do I find him? Well, we don't want to pursue this any further. Or it'll pursue us. How does one make a free being, who needs no credit, no bonds, no ships: owner-, out-, or insidership, a defier, who does not pay the interests which, before his birth already, accrued, accumulated, discombobulated, ambulated and assembled at the ring in order to KO him, not to mention the worm that guards the bank's capital, a worm, a humongous one, but not in the computer!, how do I make that other being, how do I produce this human, who would no longer be me and enact from within himself whatever I want? How do I whip up such a fool? Yes, how? So many idiots, there must be one among them? I, ape, going apeshit over myself. That other I, I long for, that other, I never see, for the free man must fashion himself. And he will surely look it. Whenever I work with plasticine and knead and ring my hands and knead and knead, the outcome is always the same and that is: serfs. I want to create one who resembles God, but I don't nail it. He actually should have been on top of the cake for the double wedding, but the way he looks I can't expect a taker. No, no comparison will make *you* safe, because the hero will have to guile- guilt- debt- and doubtlessly assume my debts and die. The little figure high up on top of the *Torte* will not be comparable to him, he will more or less resemble a candied cherry, I think. Maybe I'll still manage arms and legs, but certainly not hands and feet, those are damned difficult. The cherry'll stay on top of the *Torte* and the serf, my serf will just keep laughing and throw his life behind him like cherry pits. Then I'll no longer have one. Then I'll be serf to myself, other serfs, also to my very self, will certainly no longer come here. The last flight came in. There won't be another. I don't want to delude myself, because that's exactly what I want. That others willingly want what I want. That someone comes along, in a small middle-class bank, why not, for God's sake – for myself, to whom the dramatic changes at the global financial markets did not remain hidden. So now he is here and doesn't know what to do, he only knows he must do something. The core business is always a chore, but I removed the core before I tried to create the small human figure, because the core business was insufficient. What on earth was the result? A hero who wants to create returns on equity, the likes of which are not customary here? And whoever wants to make such profits, will also need products which are not customary here. Those products he creates out of nothing the same way I created humans. Except that I was more successful, of course. My sustainability was larger. Humans still exist, after all. The hero muses. He can't count but he wants to achieve a better bank balance sheet and if he can't do this, he must dress up the old one, adorn the bride, put the cherry on top of the cake, put the ring to work, as a lever, any which way that works. The cherry, however, which was intended as a human figure, can only get up there with a ladder. Or he must finally steal the ring, he knows where it is after all. And lo and behold, he's got it! It's been on his finger all the time! So he doesn't have to go far! Way to go! Across the board a banker's bravado. He's got the ring, he's got the *Schatz*, he's founded the Rhineland Fund, based: Channel Island Jersey, my favourite Greens land!, name: Loreley, there she sits and sings, there ships sail and sink. Because an upstart hero from the Rhineland sat down on her, so

44

the barge, the bark got overloaded, like your writing, exactly like your writing, child! There you see what happens when you write too much or when the hero sets sail and doesn't know whereto. He definitely sits too low, that low roller. Yes, and the horse was on it too. The horse was ferried along, Rhineish screw makers and similar dwarfs twisted it in such a way that the barge held up. They've got to make some money too, but it doesn't work with their screws, whoever does the screwing doesn't get them in. They might ground the ship, just on the grounds that the stockholders want more. This screw brings nothing. The lever will bring it in. No, the lever won't bring it in either. One would have to screw elsewhere, one would have to lever out someone else. The bank's core business is still too strenuous, even though the money also works very hard. The margins are pitiful. Why don't we steal the whole bank then, Papa?, you once asked. I don't know, child. I really didn't know. Greedily I held the gold. Fifteen per cent tax for capital gains. Albeit not here with us! Well, we haven't got that, but we've got something similar which in the end always means that one pays nothing. I, God!, mind you, gets paid nothing. But the State doesn't get what's his either. They think just because they don't see me, they don't have to pay the mortgage. They think, just because they want to get in on the real estate market, it will get them something! That building thing was on the wrong track. The straight track gets you close, but still no cigar. You just have to roam through the woods, there's enough work there without it being called that. Trees are also work, even when they fall. Houses are also work before they collapse. That man is protected from my revenge only by what I made. My sword. The ironclad weapon. Nothing will come of it any more. It will be packaged like the rope of the Norns, the daughters of the Earth, I mean, the norms, the daughters of humans: first they twist the rope and, whatever is in the rope – if it isn't yourself who's hanged himself – gets bundled and traded, it is the Nothing that gets traded and you can tell that that's what it is. It looks like nothing and it is nothing. But people don't believe it. The Nothing gets bartered. And the biggest Nothing is love. No one gives anything for it, no one gets anything for it. Who's interested in it? Not even a god. No, wrong, everybody is interested in it. It costs nothing, after all. And yes, what I love I must leave, you too, my child, you won't even notice, there's nothing to it, and you'll sleep anyway. I have a soporific effect. It's the only way. I can't stand by the laws I made myself. I would have to follow them myself. The laws stand, I never stand still. Only you are subject to them, unfree humans, the laws of interests and compound interests you must succumb to, the bank, in the meantime, steps on the gas some, but it doesn't get any further, it stays put, I think in Düsseldorf, yes, that's where it stays, it doesn't know where to go and it doesn't know where to put the money, it's getting less and less while it should get more and more, it does it wrong and it accelerates more and more, but it finds itself in the wrong terrain, nothing works any more, the more gas the less *Geld*, the more *Geld* the less the gas should be stepped on. The government steps in, the government steps out, it speeds up, it slows down, all of you might as well give up and lie down! And that's what you'll do now, child. Fall asleep! That's a good idea, mine, of course, I've been there, after all, when the bank and the State get moving and not in the same direction. They do it wrong. Whatever one does, it's a no-win situation. Show me a possibility to overpower those gods, and I am one of them and I will seize it. But there is none. Not even for me. Lie down, get some rest. Everything I built must collapse. I will it such. Let the insurances pay, why not, but let it all collapse. Let something new emerge, I just don't know what. But one thing I know: without me. And only one thing I want: the end. Now get some rest, child. Rest right here, allow yourself some quiet and peace! Yes, you I am talking about! Actually, I destined that you should sleep carefree and and not just forever. That which rests, rusts. But you shall rest nonetheless. Helmet and harness, yes, also you two! What rusts, rusts. At the moment I can't think of anything else for you. Because you'll never come clean with love, I can see that already. As a member of my army you probably learned only to destroy. Love is a fallacy! It dies as it emerges, like capital dies if it does not bear interest. Then it gets consumed, due to itself, by itself, like love. A capital that does not yield or pay interest, paid by the debtor, would mean to extend oneself beyond that bill of exchange and any necessary change! A mutual guarantee, not for costs, not for profit, then crash at some point in the course of change which one simply has to accept, but even then, debt is still written on the bill of exchange. Sure. You think it is so easy to acquire love? Nothing is easy to acquire, if one is tight, I mean if one becomes too tight on oneself, if one becomes tight-fisted. If one doesn't pay the interest to oneself, doesn't forgive those of others either, if one forgets them, loses interest, then nothing is left, for anyone. As fanatics of the valorization of values we relentlessly force others into production, if we are in the fortunate position to produce products, I am rather for stealing, as everyone knows, still, producing goes on, like in love, for the sake of production. Everyone wants it, everyone thinks he needs it, but he doesn't need it. Love, he doesn't need it at all. One fellow even sacrificed himself, for love, but for him it had to be for the whole world! Arrogant prig! I never could stand that saviour! The individual's full, free development through love, through work, through the workforce, by being more appealing than others? A natural quality, which, however, does not grow naturally, like capital. Only as the personification of capital are we gods in the mansion on the hill acceptable. We improve the conditions of production, the others exhaust themselves under them, we extort, I mean exhort, others are exhausted, there are always some who are exhausted, until our capital is exhausted as well. Sleep! You shall sleep, child. Those who sleep earn nothing and deserve nothing. Asleep, you don't sin and incur no debts. Love, the only product everyone thinks he needs, is the debt! You pay and pay but you don't even make the interest payment. You keep paying, but love doesn't even work as an eye-opener. It doesn't work at all, it is blind and dumb, love is. It's there but it does nothing and can't do a thing. It has the choice to come, go or stay. That's quite simple, but it can teach you fear, which is not something you absolutely need. If you ask me, I don't need it. He who is marked has it coming. Go and ask brother tree. So it is. He who hits the mark on the market has it made, except if he hit on the wrong countries. No, no, it'll all go well. And if we are allowed to love, we don't have to come out at all. But that stupid love, so unpredictable, can't ever count on it. It makes no difference, though, whether unpredictable or miscounted, as happens mostly. Either it's there or it isn't. Check out this dating site. Not for *you*? Then take a look at that one. Not your thing? Keep going. Take a walk with the eyes and if *you* only have one, use that one. Right there I just saw another one emerging from the site like smoke, like fog! It can't be a fire, I wouldn't know what would burn there. Still, hurry up, or *you'll* come too late for your satisfaction, you dick. You can't desire not to do something. And acquiring love, how could that work at all? Better not even try. Buy? When one's heart is breaking, yes, also for the love of the child, what can one do? That's like a river breaking out. How can one stop it? If it's too late too quickly? No one there to turn to? Everything must crumble and die and decay and get wrecked, everyone must croak, raging desire, burning pain, I won't save anyone, let alone with my lips, child, not you either. Someone else must do that. I won't save anyone. Done, gone. And you, who saved heroes, now you will be lined up by me all the way in the back, for if you don't displace someone, you will be displaced, just like every, absolutely every kind of human labour. Behind every worker there's already another one who does it cheaper. The capitalist cuts nonetheless, even though they all worked so diligently, so now he cuts something and it won't be his profits, there always was someone who worked for even less then the one before him. This rope must not be clipped, this drugstore chain must not be disrupted, the next one undercuts the previous one, ask the aforementioned brother tree, no, not that one, I don't know whom you could ask, but the last one ends up with nothing, that is the logical consequence of this sequence, okay, he doesn't have nothing, but he always has too little. The lover, juiced just a moment ago, jolts: does he, she, have someone else? That's always a possibility. It doesn't show. Jesus of Nazareth – also a great wanderer, albeit never alone, the guy could never be alone: a god like me. But whereto, why? I am she, whom you seek, says the Nazi bride, whom no one believed or trusted earlier, on the telephone, when she called the police emergency line. She tells them exactly what Jesus told his captors. Trust means bust. Wedlock is deadlock. Exactly: these are the words of Jesus. For everyone can say anything. No one's got to act. The capitalist's right to exist, his only right is, that 'he not have no date'. That's a quote, I don't understand it myself, I don't even know how I could find it. Yes, I admit, it sounds weird, but that is how it's been said, I even simplified it, but I don't get it even in that form. 'I not have no expiration date.' God and money, they not have no expiration date-siphon either, wherein they could simply vanish – gargle, gargle, gone. What do they all want then from love? That it remains, as the only thing left, is what they want from love. Well, many don't want this, but they all want love itself to remain, what else is left for it than be left. Money is easier to predict, you can't contradict me in this, child. Everything can be calculated, but it never adds up. Something is wrong at the bottom line. The instruments get tuned, the tools get shown, but nothing is right. What's right is that nothing is right. The advanced value was a shot in the dark, it hardly added value. It hardly produced surplus value, money did not transform into capital, capital not into gold, gold not into the hoard, where it can be stored in peace and quiet. That man did not transform into a lover, even though he had every opportunity. Why should he have shot around with himself all over the place, the lover, why should he have senselessly hit the one he didn't want to hit on. Why get her of all possible options? The capitalist: why then would he have shot his money all over the place? Until everyone was dead? How then should it ever become more, for him? And all the clients are dead now too? Oh dear, that would be too bad. Whether he buys the house, the

fortress for himself and his spouse, all finished or cus-
tom-built, by giants or dwarfs, all of whom also want to
outsmart each other, whatever, none of these doings will
increase the money spent on the acquisition of this
house. So there. Can't eat money. Not even these golden
apples: they are not edible, are only to look at and for
one's youth, which one gave to make more from it, I
mean, to make more of oneself. The apples make the investment in youth unnecessary. Therefore, look for
other options. Youth is taken care of. A write-off. From
youth still more youth! What's the point of that? That
too must end. It can't go on forever. Where there is nothing, the god lost his right he himself defined, wrote,
signed off on, signed. What's there for me to do now?
What's there for us to do now? Where's the surplus value? How will it work out, turning money into capital,
which then will walk alone, wandering through the
world, like myself, Wotan, moody and blind, not even
one-eyed!, blind!, one-eye are you sleeping; you should
have gotten off before, now it's too late! Still got to go another stop, another season for the skiers among us! It
used to be easier, when work was still done for individual people for money. Now money works on its own,
without supervision. And love does nothing. It just waits
for others to protect it, it can't do anything. The girls in
the Rhine, whom could they stop! You, my daughter,
must not stop the dying hero, because he gets what he
wants, in contrast to the gods who get what they don't
want and they must want what they don't want, I keep
saying this again and again. Not your problem, child. I
am not saying that you are a problem child. The daughters let everything run through their fingers, no wonder,
since they are living in the water and don't know anything else! The treasure belongs to them. Your treasure

does not belong to you, daughter. Your *Schatz* will change into an object of hate, because love must always change and always for the worse. No matter, man expires anyway. Makes no sense to hang on to him. Who says so? Everyone can say his treasure belongs to him. The treasure belongs to anyone who piled it up. No, not to anyone who earned it. Not everyone deserves a treasure. Because the normal quality of labour factors does not depend on the worker, it depends on the capitalist. He creates the labour, he offers it and then he takes everything that comes out at the bottom. He takes the whole shitload. It belongs to him. He takes everything. He takes everything from everybody. The money already belonged to him before. He takes it again when it has become more. Now the money is called capital. Living labour power gets no longer incorporated in its dead materiality. Good quality gets no longer incorporated in the goods. Its dead materiality is no longer imbued with living labour power. The goods are no longer imbued with good quality. The power no longer does anything, it is no longer needed; whatever will appear, it won't be pretty, good thing it will be transformed, completely without humans, it will be transformed without commodities, without goods, it will be transformed, without goodness, without zest, without anger, it will be transformed, it will be transformed into value: past, objectified, dead love, dead, dead, dead labour, consumed labour, labour given away, abandoned labour, orphaned labour, labour left behind, everything that lives, everything that is, everything that will be, everything that is dead, will be transformed into capital, value adding value out of and to itself, an animated monster that begins to work as if it still had love in his body. But love is a machine and, at some point, it will break. Everything that's made, breaks. Everything else too. And thus you go to sleep, child, having love in the body, but you can't keep it, because money exists exactly because one can't keep it. Only very few know how to do it. So, how are you doing? Well, thank you. Can't complain. Yes, money's got it all right. It got it that only a few can keep it. As soon as you get it, it gets ripped out of your hands. Look at the screen! Look, the shining numbers that call the price of the *Schatz*, but never shall you pay it, always shall you ask it, but never ever pay it. Nobody pays, they all just take in, but they don't know what they take. They borrow money to buy something they won't even own but rather sell again as soon as its value increased. They already look to the day after tomorrow, they don't even want to know what happens. They already look to whom they can sell what they had bought on credit but didn't own. They love, but they don't even take a closer look at who or what. They've got it, but they don't know why, they only know that someone else must have it when it increased in value. They don't know what. They know nothing. They let it slip through their fingers. They let other people on boards, in cars, in airplanes, on ships slip-slide away, just go go go, the main thing is, loss go away, so that more can be got, okay, not everyone go away, not just everything goes!, some also keep what they think is theirs. But they don't really want it. They want it to belong to someone who would pay them still more for it, for something they never owned, I won't say who is who. They keep it in any case, even if it's nothing. No wonder, they all are so hot for the treasure, that everyone wants to outwit the already scattered guards. The treasure wanders but no one can keep it. It is not intended for the process of creating money that in the end the treasure lands where it started, without having expanded and all others are dead instead. That only the treasure is there, albeit not its owners, oh well, we can do without them, but not without prices having risen, and if it's just a bump on the ground, it still is some elevation, isn't it, so then, the treasure. It now had gone so far, for so long, that it is again where it started out, that's another term for been stolen, when the prices were still low. This treasure is no steal for anyone, but it gets stolen all the time. It is a heck of a steal and does get stolen constantly. The heroes sink to the ground. Those who are not heroes also sink. It makes no difference to death. Only the hoard, the treasure remains, no rise in the market, no resale on better terms, it belongs to this one, then to that one, its guardians change, it gets thrown in the water and then pulled out again, as the case may be. It doesn't make it any better but no worse either. It stays and is guarded, or it gets carried around and also guarded. It should actually work, but it rather lies in the putrid water or in the putrefactive cave. Once it is simply forgotten by a hero, really? Cross my heart, completely forgotten by the hero. Hands reach for it, for the possession, because only possession gives a person the right, which until now the person conveyed to the possession on his own. Thus the possession is the right now, the ring is the possession, the treasure is the ring, the ring was the treasure, the possession is the right, it doesn't set right, it is it, and everything that is the law as of now, derives from it. Whoever shares in it – there should be as few as possible, it should be united in one single hand, nice and overseeable, so that its contenders can calmly smash each others heads for it, thus, whoever shares in this union, no matter between whom, is considered the natural pillar of power, of the public power. The one who shares in it might be weak, unless he holds the right shares. Love? It's the right way to share, but when it was our turn, the gods' turn, we rejected this kind of sharing. We wanted a better return. We already had each other, after all, and besides us, there was no one else. What a boring order! Directed against the law of nature, which aims for movement, which wants something to become more or less, depending on who it is. We are dead. As gods we have died for humans, and they are right. This death from order, which doesn't even need subordination, as this scale has no marks, it's not even a common ruler, this death through rigidification basically takes away my power, which would not have to be based on property, but I want the property to come with it, I want more, I wander, but I do not move, I fuck women, but I don't move doing so, I want everything, I wander, but I can't move, personally, I no longer want love, I would have to move then, but otherwise, I want it all, the property, the only thing that, except for the gods, doesn't move either, okay, the prices that quote the nothing, prices for more than there is, for more than even exists, prices for the more and the less, no matter, if everything existed that gets traded, the earth would collapse under it, it would be too much, the money alone, that wanders around like me, like Wotan, is already much too much, the prices for nothing – because more than it can give is nothing – the prices move, but not the property, even though the property is rather small compared to quotes which imply that there must be much more than there is, so there, and I still have to pay for my house which just about stretches the heavens to the limits. Everything for this *Immobilie*, this immovable real estate, as the name says already. The builders, the only ones who actually moved about busily, want something for their work. Inconceivable to me, I could, after all, have created this house out of nothing, like other gods, but in the Iron Age iron should be promoted, I understand. Thus I must pay. With still more metal, which isn't very movable either, except if it comes under the hammer. Metal was once tied to papers, contracts. Not any more. So then, how now? Could my power be honoured only by property or my property by my power? Must money get tied to gold again, which it just escaped so that it can multiply even faster?, money broken out of its chains, like a fugitive animal? I am God, albeit that many already claimed to be it. I am the only one who can prove it, here, right here is the paper I signed in person. Actually, it is a piece of wood, which cannot move in the wind. I assert myself as God, I can accomplish that, I am my own possession and the gold is also my possession. And the possession is not property, because it is so much that no one could own it any more. The gold. The gold from the river. It has a totally youthful face, always, the face on one side, on the other there's something too, money is always young, just as the beloved stays young for us forever. On both sides of the coin, which no one sees any more, no one holding it in the hand: forever young. It is always new. It doesn't age. And the people who produce it, the dwarfs who hoard it, I see them only as appearances of the distribution of their labour power to the various investment areas of capital, but the capital is just lying there. Funny that it is only a few who know that. It's simply too much. It wanders about. No one can have it any more. It is too much, there is too much of it, but practically no one's really got it. It is debt, it is interest, it is credit, everyone has debts, many receive interest, many have credits, but money they don't have. The money, rather, takes a walk, but not with you. There it lies, no, not there, you are looking in the wrong place!

No wonder, but I wonder what wonders should have been worked. It walks and it lies there simultaneously, the capital. It wanders like I do, but at the same time it just lies around albeit not with everyone. Love also wanders after all. Is it just us who keep our feet on the same ground? Yes, no one's pulling the carpet out from under our feet! We don't have to blast off right away, like that completely off-his-rocket Jesus, the saviour decided his self-sacrifice out of love for humankind, his papa agreed right away, that's how he finally got rid of him, the Spirit was silent as always, and humans had it coming, also right away, everything's always right away, so now they've got him on their plates. And I? A god who once wanted to live, wants nothing but his own downfall any more. The money wants nothing. It's there. It is *Dasein*, 'being there' itself. Living in blissful solitude, in sunlit altitude, *in seliger Öde, auf sonniger Höh*. Knowing, like the god who sacrificed himself, that it continues to live in those who own it. The god only knows that he continues to live in those who believe in him. Those have eternal life, eternal money no one's got, it would simply be too much, beyond anyone's imagination. Not even a god who created everything can imagine so much of anything. He can go down and he can also want his downfall. He can will his downfall. He always betrayed everyone who trusted him and now he wants his own downfall. Yours, child, I already decided as well. You can take with you whomever you want, yes, your horse too, you can take everything, the belt, the cap, which doesn't suit you, by the way, anything at all, the sword, fine with me, it doesn't belong to you, but someone will bring it to you, who earlier will have hammered around on it for hours on end. A good artisan, just not very intelligent. If you like yourself in this outfit, I won't stand in your way.

That's our advantage over money. We take as much as we can. But there is always too much around of which we don't know what it does when it isn't with us. No one can take it along, but it can take itself along. A fetish that follows its own rules. It carries itself, not delivered by some postal carrier, it wears on and out, as something desired. The eternal gods, however, can also keep it, eternally, as the flow runs. If humans created a god for themselves, he surely would not look like me. Old, handicapped, henpecked, one eye only, slouch hat, walking with a cane, oh well, awe-inspiring somehow? Two ravens agreed, for a horrendous wage, to escort him. Thus people think animals also obey him, yes, wolves too. Ditto that little woodbird talking nonsense. Love? Fine with me. Now sleep, child! Now, under the gods' pressure you succumb to repression, where everything inexplicable ends up, so now you get repressed, away with you, push it away, behind the flames, whatever it is, displace, re-press it behind the fire curtain. An entire branch will then be able to live off it. The money won't run out, it will walk, it will wander around the world, but it won't run out, why should it, there is nowhere it could experience more than what it finds in itself. It wasn't me, your own painful disappointments got you to where you must sleep now and that the fire is everywhere now. You shouldn't have taken offence with me. I am the biggest offence-taker, that is like one who gives the big orders but there's no one there to take them. The offence-takers also get eaten up by their disappointments. All devour or get devoured. Some devour themselves. To any 'must' they must be forced, even to their own wants. About worries they must worry. For war they must war each other. For lust they must sate each other, for other bodies they must scuffle, while others, will-lessly, care, for themselves, for everything, for nothing. All this I had originally planned for you, but ultimately it didn't work. And it won't ever work, I can see it now, even though it is a one-eyed reach of vision. It didn't work so far to get you will-less, want-less, child. And now you already want something else! Not work, not wander, but want, want, want. Even though they had such horrible experiences with it, they all want the same thing, love and money. Money or love, no, money or life, no again. Money and love, that's what they want. And love nothing better than taking the partner along into the grave. And if they die themselves in the process, they don't care, they can't give away what they've finally got. You don't seriously want that, child? You want to want that? You want what they all want? You don't want it? Well, Papa will teach you, if you want nothing. You must want something, and naturally it must be something your father also wants. You won't get it, you know that, but you must want something! No. Nothing. Only your fingers are moving nicely, beating out the words, who will now take on this guilt without guilt, well, someone else will do that, you'll get to meet him for sure, that other one, who will be like you, just different, it'll certainly be an idiot, a dodo, an anal impaler, only that kind of guy will go through fire, I can see it already, how stupid must one be for that, doesn't matter, if he wants it that way. Instead of throwing away that ring, he will throw away his whole life like a piece of scrap metal with a most unique ring on it for the purpose of opening the can, opening up the virgin, the can, the worthless colourful metal, no, not even that, the worthless tinplate cans with aluminium mixed in, which not even the supermarket will take back, correction, I do know better: which every supermarket takes back, because every, absolutely every can they can get their hands on gets recycled, that's why we've got them, that's what they are for, so that every can can be made into a new one, maybe even two? It is the miraculous multiplication of cans, maybe, they can be squashed, but most use their fist: the can is *Dreck*, filled with *Dreck*, but if it is sick, tired or empty, it can be restored again, attacan!, the best there is here in this muck, this slime, this mud, better the can than the toxic, sticky goo that's in it. Well, the idiot, the dodo, the twit, the dick, the moron, the pussy fart, the cum guzzler, the clit mouse, the thundercunt, the pucciaca, the fucktoy, the fuck-goes-with everything, what are they all going to do now, after they drank it all, until they drip themselves, yes, still talking about the can? Some other guy stands there already, he pulls the flap, lowers his mouth and slurps something that consists mainly of sugar, gas and assets, no, acid. A can filled with sugar and exhaling, and there he goes!, guzzle, guzzle, going gaga... The ring that's been opened by this magnificence – which is due only to magnifi-gents – he will keep the ring and instead throw his sweet, active life behind him. No, the other way around. He'll throw something. So. That's the one who shall come to save you. Well, you'll be in for something, my child! The ring means more to him than his life. The ring means as little to him as this object which once was a can and the object, a surplus value had also flowed into, in the form of Cola, Fanta or Sprite or that energy Bull or whatever, which had the labour of people flowed in, is worth more now than the can has been, which was nothing whatsoever, even though its parts were forged in fire, like the ring, just like it. We draw a conclusion for the lid and body of the can, we determine the aluminium content, we can do all that, but it lost its useful quality, the fluid as product, caught in

60

bright gloss, the fluid's been drunk, the can is not well, it is empty and crushed, but a person, after all, had pressed his value constituent part onto the product!, dear can body: iron, dear can lid: aluminium, with a flap, a hole in the middle for *Rheingreifen* forget it, stupid joke – as all my jokes, *you* guys keep writing – sunk in the Rhine, lost in translation, on we go! The dwarfs made a beautiful ring out of the gold and what do *you* do with your cans?, the means of production have been raised from the dead and for the dead, you are not dead yet, my child, you are sleeping, like the entire labour power, sleeping, so, fall asleep already!, a huge sleeping crowd pursuing specific activities, which don't do them any good, yet others get the goods instead, at least I hope so, yes, such human activity thus raises, by mere contact, the means of production from the dead and a product emerges, here, this one, for example. Halleluiah! What did I want to say? A product, an object, *Dreck*, a dream, endless, the end is not priced in and not programmed, those products, which were made and are still in the making even as we speak. You, however, will sleep until the hero comes, who then, some day, well, not some day, I decide when, will get the spear in the back, I would have assumed you had a bit more knowledge of human nature, child, but you, taking him of all prospects – no! That was stupid. He is stupid. But then, any other one would also die. The hero can be handed a means of production, but better just a product, only one at a time, which he can wreck, but not a human being. That's common knowledge. The hero, in his surplus time, that's left to him between his deeds, will not produce value or money. He will ponder his next deeds and unfortunately, also execute them someday, you can take that to the bank, no, better take your sleeping schnaps or your constant benzodiazepine. You can barely escort him to Walhalla, the hero, but it will start burning right away. Like everything the hero touches, and were it out of love, everything will burn, mark my words. The anti-capitalist demo, the millionth one will be promoted and occur. The occupation will be set up as a sit-in. But it will bring them as little as all the others, because no bets are set on the sitting, the beset, those without assets. They do nothing. They don't move. Who cares? Only the movement of money counts. Whoever wants to bring everybody something, that is, nothing, it'll bring them nothing, but that won't add up, there is too much already, so much so, that nothing will be traded, the main thing is to act, to borrow, even though there is too much, one wouldn't even have to buy it, it is far too much, after all, stocks will fall, because no one gets their heads stuck in them any more, that's summer stock shtick these days, they'll rather stick to their guns. Stock prices will fall, because altogether there is too much of everything and slowly it's getting too much for everyone, you can bed your ass on it, there will be so much money, one can sit on it, what did I want to say, the values, however, will only be borrowed, even though there is so much worth, and then they will be sold, the values, yes, but only when they dropped, I don't understand any of it anyway, still, I am writing it: even though there is so much of it that the worth, the money, the values don't find a place to sit down, they will only be borrowed, not bought, even though there is so much, one could give them away, they will be resold, even though they weren't even bought, just borrowed, well, okay, there will be fees, not much, but still, if the bet on the values works out, the money can be bought at a more decent price, still lower than before and then returned to the lender as less, always less than it was, although there was too much of it and still is, you pay with something you don't have yet, to one who doesn't need it, but hopes it will get more, however, if it doesn't, you still have to repurchase it, the zeroes are on a chase, only the zeroes must run, if you can, you must purchase, only the zeroes must chase one after the other; too few shall have too much, too many shall have too little, no, that must not be like that any more, everyone shall have less, though everyone has less, no one too much, it shall be more equitable, everything shall run more equably, the periodic fructification of capital shall come to all, everyone shall be permitted to pick our golden apples, but no, that wouldn't bring anything to anyone, it will always be others having it all. I declare this still uncounted demo opened, the police say half, we double the half, regarding the number of participants it will be true, but it is superfluous anyway, the demo, as I, herewith, also declare all those superfluous as superfluous. I could also declare them fluid and stuff the gold into them, throw it into them, exactly, it might as well be thrown away, I could declare them the river Rhine which always flows, in it a sluggishly labouring treasure which, however has already been taken by a worm into his cave, where he already tramped it down. The boy who's got no patience will just leave it there, he's got other priorities, he kills everyone who keeps him from assessing treasures, but leaves the treasure behind. That's not how I want it: the largest part of the poor shall never be idle and then they shall get nothing for it, but still spend it. But you can't force the poor to 'must', they have nothing to lose, after all. They only live as long as they can find work and they only find work as long as work increases the capital. But that's no longer true for today, because capital multiplies by itself. I could throw the money to the poor, but would it bring anything? Would they, who spend their lives eking out a living, still have the incentive to keep still in their laborious zeal?, wouldn't that drive them to a works meeting, to strike?, it would bring nothing. A zero-sum game, where the zeroes get a little bit, not nothing, a little bit, exactly as much as they can spend. The capital does the rest on its own. Fainthearted by contrast and little motivated is the worker: it'll always be others who act otherwise. Brazen and lazy, as soon as he owns something that goes beyond his way of life, which he then will deny. He will contest it to the end. But meanwhile it doesn't matter whether he is brazen or lazy or humble or gets humiliated. He will contest that he's got to work more than he absolutely has to. That's what it'll lead to. If a god can quit his job and wish for the end, a worker can quit much sooner. Wherever slaves are prohibited already, almost everywhere these days, the gigantic mass of the hardworking poor will replace them and represent the actual wealth. No, wealth alone will represent wealth. It will check out the stockyards and then it will represent the stocks. The hero will represent god, but the god won't be able to represent the hero, though he will be able to produce the hero. The hero as well as the worker will do with what they will get. Each will be remunerated according to the collective agreement, so that he is able to satisfy his needs, which are always those of others. It will always be others and it will always be everything they want. The one-family house of the gods, uninsured of course, who would insure gods!, who would reinsure themselves against them!, yes, everything uninsured and everything will burn down now, finally justice for all, for all the workers also got burned. Everything burns. You too, you will burn too, child, your hero will burn, you will burn, though I don't really understand why everything must burn, just because of a negligible theft, not really a break-in, a minor incident, the Rhine is always open, around the clock, no one locks it up, these are mitigating circumstances, it's not robbery. Well, if that's not robbery what's been done with the gold, then I don't know any more. And robbery was followed by robbery followed by robbery followed by robbery. Greedily we held on to the gold. This doesn't mean though that it'll be standard, that the gold standard can be reintroduced. That's over. Gold is the standard only for us gods and we spent it on our home. But we also got something for it! It's burning now, the roof burns, the hat burns. Everything burns. Why everything has to burn for it is beyond me. Okay, thus a god turns away from you, child. But still there won't be an end for you. At least there won't be a happy end. For me, the wanderer, it will be. Soon. But it won't be fun. I don't care. I am no longer attached to anything. Finally, death does come in the end, because life also comes to an end, so death comes to an end! For you, your hero will come and it will be death, it is what heroes always are.

B: Father, what to say to a child who does not understand herself? I didn't do anything. In fact, I did nothing else than what you did! When the milk teeth fall out, we advance ourselves with ourselves, chess pieces, which leave their own hand, before they can strike, before they can beat another figure. I see you in fear, you, a god, relative of gods, father of demigods, and I see in you fear, because you rule by treason! You might seem powerful to the unfree, but not to me. But I must obey you. Only my hero will free himself from it. I don't know him yet, but he certainly will get to know me!, he won't

know what hits him, he never does, but he doesn't need
to, he only needs the will, he will defy you, also your
relatives, he'll defy everybody, he will fight, he'll want
to give away everything, eventually, he will also betray:
me. He won't know it. He will act unconsciously and
that will also be your fault, Papa. Not his fault, yours!
Maybe mine too. I might not be up to this love, I won't be
able to be Jesus or Antigone. I won't be able to cross you
once again, just because of the bit of ground that marks
the shore, anything can cross that line, even the river,
I won't break your law, it did me no good the first time,
all it got me was a long night's sleep. The hero was laid
next to me, just like that, as a burial gift. I'll never come
to terms with the hero, because we can't exist on equal
terms. The hero will die, the curse will do him in. I too
will do him in, done in by your army, I've never seen
anything but arms, and this won't be a woman's weapons, with those shoes?, never!, and my skirt will always
be too long, never sexy, because of my legs. My love will
then turn into hate. My understanding will become a
misunderstanding, no matter with whom I talk. I will
go to waste and I will waste others. I'll want their end.
I will be jealous, because the jealous one is always zeal-
ous, always on the look-out, looking down to the ground
that is, it hides his face, which would tell all, he has arrived at rock bottom now, with the cockroach cooks,
the veggie scratchers, the slaves, he burrows in filth, the
jealous one, I will kill the hero, either way, friendship,
says the socialist, if only to his kind, I, however won't
be looking for friendship, only hate, jealousy, death, I
will wreck everything, also the hero who was sent to
me, I will wreck him, before he wrecks me. Wreck what
wrecks you, yes. You guys up there. You gave me the
idea! I am the one who wrecks the Redeemer and does

not get redeemed for it. What do you care? I am no longer one of you. We down here, we want to trade, but not
with ourselves, we are better, but not batty. It must not
be as if we were the means of payment for ourselves, but
not our own masters. Gold pays with itself. That's not
our business. The hero pays with himself. This will be
my personal business. And how I deemed myself your
beloved, Father! For eternities! Why? Only your farewell words explained it to me. *Flammende Glut umhülle
den Fels mit zehrenden Schrecken*, to wit, fiery flames encircle the rock with all-consuming fright and so on and
so forth, no, not forth. It's all forthcoming, I am getting
ahead of you, because I can't get away from here, it is
as if I got into smoke. Your favourite lover is what I'd
have liked to have been, but you always were with another one. Yes, also with Mama. With Mama deep down
in the earth. I wanted to be that too, for the hero, one
always wants what one practised, but it never works,
practise as much as you want, it doesn't work when it
counts. The hero's lover. But he too will score with another one. He could score with any woman. Things will
be rotten in the state of the Rhineland, but then, what
doesn't rot sooner or later? All that is, all that will be,
ends – my sisters told me so before, but I didn't listen. I
always know better. I am the light, but only when it gets
lit, the truth, but only when it is told, how else would one
know what it is, and life, but only when it comes to an
end. Whoever loves me, follows me, whoever loves you,
Father, follows your orders and you follow your wife's.
She is what today they call a strong woman, I can't hear
it any more, an independent woman, I can't hear it any
more. I can't hear anything that comes up with woman.
The woman either comes or she doesn't come. Thus God
comes to an end, but nothing begins. It really ends. How

pitiful, how pathetic. I felt like the sky was falling on me from your castigations, Father. You are telling me, from whom I should take the sword and to whom I should give it, but we won't need a sword for that, no matter whether we put it between ourselves or in the drawer on the kitchen table. Completing the household utensils, those useful companions. It just comes pelting down on me. Once spilled tea on the nightstand, I was sick, horrible punches, all over me. How sick is that, Father? I felt like the sky was falling on me. Compared to that, this is tame, sleeping behind flames, big deal, having one's peace, finally peace and quiet!, others sleep much more uncomfortably, and those flames give warmth at least, that's their upside. But they've also got different ways.

W: (*makes fun of her*) Woe, woe, valla, valla, wail, like your mama! Papa loves another one, how terrible! Papa doesn't love you, so follow someone else, I am no heaven crashing on you. I know, just anybody isn't enough for you, it has to be the One, but you won't know that there is no other one and that is because you won't get another one. And in the end, he will turn out to be the second one who will take a second one, after you. He will be moved up, he will have to line up behind himself. He will redeem an injustice, that's at least something, someone will redeem it, he'll pay all right, also with himself, an injustice no one will remember. No property you could steal, with which you could walk off. A ring on your finger, nothing else is what you want, like all women! I know! A pawn no one redeems. You want a ring to have something to show off with. Papa doesn't love you! How terrible! And there you yammer endlessly, such an embarrassing experience! Papa thrashed you and now he creates a fire around you to boot! But now everything's on fire. Unfortunately, the insulation is also burning, which it isn't supposed to. Can't rely on anything any more. It should actually prevent everything from burning. And there it is also on fire! No wonder you can't prevent your jealousy in your old hate, child. We gods owe our entire wealth to the work of others, but we also had to pay for it, albeit against our will. And then our house burns down, because the giants used the wrong insulation, polystyrene for the polymorphous who keep defrauding others in manifold shapes. Even as a worm. Serves them right, and the right also comes from them. So. Then everything burns because you can't control yourself. Then everything burns because the kids played with fire, no, not because of that, the gods have no children, their children are grown up already at birth. The gods save themselves a lot because they don't have to save. I don't think you also have to return the ring, but, if you must...! I just don't see that you absolutely have to. I sent you the hero. And what are you doing with him? You are jealous because of him. Right from the start, when there was no other woman. And right away the next phase of development sets in, that's a safe bet with you, while I am waiting for you to finally quit writing. Time to stop working, *Götterkind*, divine child! Instead you always start tackling something new, attacking unliked types who are loved all the more elsewhere. You start hate campaigns while you are sleeping. And you call that work! Your dependency on writing is, as any expert knows, necessary for your wellbeing and you doing anything at all. You can't do anything else. Ridiculous. Except no one cares what you do. Arms make the man – it won't ever happen do you. It would be easier if someone would finally loosen your helmet: that's not a man! I am so sorry for you, child! He'll notice right away, I am sure. And immediately he'll call for his mother to help him. Hail to you sun, hail to you light he will sing, but he'll see neither sun nor light. He will name things wrongly, even if he sees them correctly, that's his problem. You too, daughter, you too will say hail, you'll say it to the Earth, who never wanted someone like you. You are a freak who, awakened, only sees her hero. Got eyes for nothing else, the daughter. I let you sleep, but not forever. You wake up and right off you are what you always were: not a man! Rather burning for one who applies the wrong insulation against you! And everyone finds it good! Read this, read that, check out this column, check yourself: they all find it good. I am sorry for you: everyone finds it good. Sure, you can do nothing else when you are sleeping and forgot to turn off the device, from where the image comes. Wait, I'll help you with it, it is this button, it is this icon, it is this image of an image, much reduced of course, or the finger won't do, no, the finger won't die, press lightly, the finger does its job. Here, in the picture, you can see that it is right to see just one hero and no other. You have the say in whom you will see, here you have the choice, you have the say, I say! Here you can see him, if much reduced. Then you can decide if you also want him big. It's been going on for a long time, that folks get chosen when they are small and then one can't stand them big. We all want to be better off. If one wants to see anything at all, it should be a hero. Here it says how to get to the hero. This one even comes to your home. The device picked up your thoughts and, right here it spits out the hero. Here comes the hero, that's right, he himself wrote in his profile that he is no hero, which means that he most definitely is a hero. In him the light shall win that comes out of the socket onto a shining screen, in this picture the light wins, the hero wins, the winner is the one brought by wonderfilled push-button impressions, everywhere they say, this is what winners look like, now you can see for yourself, child. You knew this even before you were born. When this device didn't even exist. But now the screen is bright, if not enlightened, but pretty bright compared to a human, and the hero shows you how winners look: like him. The way he looked in the picture. And that's how he is. When you wake up and look into the light, the conquering light, the all-consuming flame, it would have been better you'd have stayed asleep. But best, if everyone fell asleep again now. Their devices stay with them. The light talks. No budget constraints for that. The light talks nonsense, but it's the only means that makes us see. It will be the only truth that we can see. *Sieg heil*, says the light, it is the thought that must not be named, because it can be seen anyway. The small image here, which can also be enlarged. And what one sees, does not have to be named any more. What is seen is always the hero. Why do anything? Why publish a book of poems, a novel, this play which is not one; he who brings something to many, brings nothing to anyone. Only what you see, exists. Without light no thought, without light, thought not needed any more. You are waiting for the titanic meeting with the hero, I can understand that, he'll come, your hero, I will send him to you, just you wait, so then confronting each other will be the landed property, the outlandish, alien property one appropriates and that is confronted by money, the monetary assets, the hoard, the *Schatz*, it gets born, *Geld*, it is debt, it is guilt, it is a hole one cannot reach into, no, can't even touch, it gets out of hands over and over again, *Geld* is blamed for someone. Always someone else, debt as guilt has long degenerated into debt as debts, but debts generated guilt again, usurer capital, merchant capital, commodities left unsold, the daughters of gods who love or are also left behind, always for someone else, always by someone else. The capital appears on stage, enter *Das Kapital*, did *you* ever think about what it should look like?, because the first time *you* see: *Das Kapital*, *you* should recognize it right away! *Das Geld*, enter the *Held*: *Dreck* compared to it, gold, debt, guilt, the same story plays every day, right in front of our eyes, no day off, we keep playing, now the capital enters the market, the commodities market, the labour market, the money market, it enters its workplace, the Rhine, it is a sort of exhibition diver who slips through everybody's hands that want to take his oxygen bottle away from him, but there, at the Rhine, I won't let it be, it belongs to me as I am not paying with it. That way it stays with me in toto. A wonder that more folks don't get the idea! I am not paying for our new house, I owe the builders their fee, but I don't pay, I increase the debt that is money, if debt is guilt is debt is money (damn right, Mark Twain, 'That awful German language!' *Schulden = Schuld = Schulden = Geld*), so, if debts are money, then it doesn't matter whether I am in debt to money or the giants, who worked for it, an ingenious way to make money, unfortunately already outdated. In debt I am anyway and guilty to boot. Capital enters the market, looks around, step right up and try your luck, it wants to – by means of certain proceedings, which it still has to start – transform into capital. Capital is more than money. Something is added to the money. If I knew what, I could take it, but the search for it has already turned into a dear habit. I have this small device with pictures for it, but when I look up a phone number, a numeral, it takes longer, I must enter something, I get something from it. So now I have to puke, it is simply too much what's been fed to me. Hello, who am I talking to? Okay. So then I might just as well pay off the giants, nonetheless, something will be coming in, something always comes after another, but there must be someone in front or at least one drilled for our kind of front; something will come that's worth more than gold, golden apples will come, that's more gold, and golden youth, that's our capital. So we can easily hand over the gold. It's play money for those who don't have to die. They also can play with other stuff. We give it to the giants who worked for it; we don't blame them for their slavish dependence, we blame them for their comfortable dependence on us, because comfort is the foremost necessity for well-being, about which we couldn't care less with regard to the giants. Let them kill each other, we'll gladly pay for it and we'll even throw something into the bargain for that. Only one left, he needs the gold. The other one needed a woman, he just didn't really know how to search for one, he didn't even quite understand this picture of a woman, but maybe he pressed the wrong icon. Now he's got nothing. His murderer doesn't have much either, but still. However, it was us who created the capital and that's more than gold. Our capital never melts and never gets consumed. It expands. It covers the whole world. So I take something whenever I want. Capital is money with something added on, is labour with something added on, is a commodity to which something's been added on already, a shot of Rhine flowed into it, but it's still good, except that it can't swim, but that doesn't matter. What it can do already is absolutely sufficient. Look, here *you* see the transformation of commodity into money and the re-transformation of money into commodity. Selling in order to buy. Something flows into the commodity, something flows into the *Schatz*, yes, the *Schatz* also flows, it flows about in the Rhine, but something also flows into the real one, the hoard, something essenceless, spectral, but on the other hand, it is also quite normal, one just has to flip it, and clear as water, once we come clean about it. It would be witless, wouldn't it, were I to give the giants the *Schatz* for their labour and the giants to give me their labour for it. So it was agreed upon, that the Earth would come up from her native cave, that is where she retreated as a plant-breeder. The business doesn't pay. The Earth we must rationalize away, no gain with her. Ur-mothers', Earth-mother's wisdom is nearing the end, their knowledge goes with the wind of our will, the Earth can also sleep for all I care, she works too little, close your eyes, Earth, something terrible will happen to your children, you better not see it. If I may advise you: down with you! Everything's earth anyway, yes, under you, not everything above you, but everything that's under you. Down you go and sleep! Can't think of anything better, Earth, for your inertia. Because everything that your beings do in you, they have to do themselves. You don't help them at all, don't even provide them with tools. You call me a stubborn savage? Really now! You aren't even stubborn, you are just lazy. You are simply there, period. That wouldn't even be enough for a god, even though it would be enough. Keeping the treasure and taking over the labour, that would be something new for once, no, nothing new, we tried it once, but then we thought of something better for buying the giants, the labour and the treasure and that is very simple, it is fraud, it is murder, it is rotten through and through, for we could definitely count on their killing each other afterwards and our counting is always right on the money; naturally, it could also be an exchange, though this wouldn't be natural, but somehow it would be, but it isn't, it is more than an exchange, it is much more, it is more than would be necessary to have something, it is as much as is necessary to get something. And then the art is, more than is necessary altogether, something nobody needs in order to get something. The art is in making money. Affluence by way of the superfluous. Making money is the greatest art of all. Having money is even better, dormant money, resting gracefully as you, child, and for dormant money fifteen per cent taxes per annum, albeit not here, to our indelible chagrin, not here. Elsewhere. That's an art, but you can't practise it here. Here you have to pay for everything. Here it's just paying, never getting. Every art always strives to push beyond its limits and for that it has to hand over only fifteen per cent per year, sadly not to us, I know, you write, child, you should know. The *Geld*, the gold is the beginning and the end. But never the same. The beginning never equals the end. Alpha never is Omega. A lot at the beginning, more at the end. Not with us. Never with us! It is like water, which has neither a beginning nor an end, insofar as it belongs in the Rhine, because you never know where it begins and where it ends. You know everything begins and ends somewhere, but with money you often don't know, with money you never know. It's impossible to know. Money. It is the root of the miraculous multiplications, whether of bread and fish as with the Saviour or of bread and wine, before the Saviour had become one. He did transform things, so that something would become more, so that there'd be more than there was before. And in the end, he gave the most: himself, the biggest sacrifice. A special idiot, no doubt. You've got to sacrifice others, never yourself. I am he whom you seek, many have said that, also those who had never been sought, but also the others who finally wanted to be found, they said it too, even though no one was looking for them. Those multiplications weave through everything, but it's not always what we want that gets multiplied. The money, the gold works on us, it wrenches us beyond ourselves, we do things we never thought possible, we never were able to do before, because money is not the means but ultimately the end and as with every art, it is limitless, this ultimate goal, it can be used for so much without one superfluous word spoken by those with surplus cash flow, in the end it should always be more than it was, get it?, unlimited is the wish for more in its drive for more, there is no barrier, there is no stop sign, there are no ten commandments or God knows how many, it's not my religion and it's not a goal either, there is nothing, there only is absolute enrichment. Unbridled appropriation. Money moves, sometimes it stumbles, but it moves and if it were in our hands, it would move in with us and never away. There is nothing that's different from money, because there is only money, there are different folks, but money comes from them only if they had it already before, otherwise they aren't all that different. Otherwise they are the same as us. We squeeze it out even from the dead, for whom we still have to pay, a small fee is due even for their graves, dead folks, whom we nevertheless can add to the heroes, so they will fight for us, even after death. That's the surplus value the dead bring us if we can deploy them, against the brother, the sister, the distant cousin who also makes claims, there's something in it for memememe, the dead no longer see what everyone knows, they go against the wind, but that's so strenuous, that they don't go anywhere. They are gone. They've always been gone. To each his own, it says right here, but each is another and one's own is not what one wants to

lose to another. The multiplication of money, of gold ad
infinitum is our goal, the goal of the living, who take it
even from the dead. Holding the treasure together,
guarding the hoard, increasing the hoard, hoarding the
money offshore and getting it back again bigger and
stronger, no matter how we do it, it must become the
most there is! Then it doesn't matter what you do. Go
ahead, talk. Talk now! Talk and tata. Speak a foreign
language, talk in tongues and toodle-oo. Talk to the animals, in their languages, at least imitate the language of
the little woodbird (but the way we hear it, it never talks,
not with its friends!) and off you go. Get your birdie in
the hole and then lickety-split. Take the money when
it'll have amassed the mostest and run. The ring, yes, the
ring, take the ring and off you go. Having money is like
living under the rule of the dead. Because gold is the
deadest there is. But death has no comparative and it
knows no return. Something I know tells me so, even
though I don't yet know it. He who knows the rights
fights the law? But what if he knew nothing whatsoever?
When sleep shuts down his knowledge? Who is this en-
tering here, one whom they murdered, a revolutionary
who, however, did nothing, my dear uncle Herrmann,
Herschel, Jellinek, I would have never thought he would
dare such a thing! I don't want to adorn myself with his
dead body, not at all, I have my own helmet, my own ar-
mour against such a thing and am going to sleep now. He
even managed a discussion with his hangman, and now
nothing is left of him, this is hard, dying at twenty-six,
what do I know about it, as for me, I sailed round this
cliff long ago and am sleeping as well. He comes out of
the earth and instantly talks nonsense, after all, they
can't kill him a second time, the dear great-grand-uncle,
but he is talking: freedom costs blood. Freedom takes

work. Oh, if the *Volk* would only know what an enormous effort it takes to create the ideas of *Freiheit*, that centuries were needed that a clear conscious quest for a specific goal could evolve. Freedom does not suddenly fall from the sky, it does not fall on the ground like a stone thrown up high, no, humans must work hard, consistently. Freedom grows back like an organic body, but what has been hacked off, doesn't grow back. Uncle Herrmann: freedom is disorder. Yes, it destroyed you too, your desire for freedom destroyed your body, or rather, it let it be destroyed, the state entrusted your body to destruction, a very friendly executioner (at least that's how I imagine him, an unfriendly one would have instantly hacked away, shot, knotted, no discussion for the sentenced, we don't have time for that, others are waiting, do you think you are the only one?!) who did not kill you without a prior discussion, without which nothing was ever possible in our family, you will get used to the pain. It is brief and joy is not eternal, at least now you haven't felt anything for a long time. And once again I throw my words into the Nothing, which will bring nothing as before, which someone will, as always, throw back at me, because this is not a business, this is a zero-sum game: destroyed must be the order that creates millions of slaves for a few! Slaves of the wealth of always others, only a few. Those few must be destroyed! I do it every day. Without consequences, like your writing, Uncle Herrmann, and you are not to blame that I am also writing. Herewith a small memorial for you; who'd be interested nowadays. You don't even want anyone to be interested. You did want it, but you know where your place is now. Not in the TV debate. There we see, for the umpteenth time, or did I imagine one having taken place?, that no one knows anything and that's why we

are working, uncle. Because working means to acknowledge the rule of the dead, yes, yours too!, the rule of the
treasure, the few who guard it or even own it. The rule of
gold, this lifeless matter, no comparison to mine, the one
I am working on, my matter has also been dead for dec-
ades. I want it all to stop, but I don't know what! I want
the useless activities to stop, that's not even what they
are or only when applied to produce more gold. I want it
to stop. I want your death to stop, Uncle, yes, yours too,
Mama, Papa and whoever else who answers voluntarily.
No, Mama, not you! My mistake. In this life, I wouldn't
want to admire your work any more. I want the following to stop, but *you* don't have to remember it and
definitely not in this order: I want the needless, the gam-
blers, gamers, industrialists, speculators, money-makers
and, in the end, money itself, it's only logical, that it
would also want to participate, so I want everything to
stop, the money also comes along, it bets, even on itself,
it turns itself into appearance, *Schein*, slips into papers to
cover its gloss, small and worthless, slips into pockets of
others and devalues everything there, money thinks
that's funny, so it stays for good, if not with us, it trans-
forms itself, it disappears, makes itself briefly invisible
and appears again in a padded envelope (so it won't hurt
itself), it's there and always there, it inscribes itself on
paper and laughs about us, it drops again into someone
else's sack and keeps laughing, can't be calmed down
any more, oh well, it will finally be able to sleep in the
bank, on a screen it attests to its own value, which it instantly devalues again, but I, I nevertheless want it to
stop, I want everything to stop, I want them all, all those
named and those who volunteered and those who will
still volunteer, they will be quite a few more, to devote
themselves to the maintenance of this state of ending

until it is all over, I want you to immediately drop everything and dedicate yourself to the increase of the More
that soils so many hands, but stays clean itself, while the
others, so many, most of them, almost all, sacrifice themselves to maintain this house of shame, which gets them
nothing. And then all of it should stop. The money
should stop running. Or it should run slower. Where
might it have dwelled? Where might it want to go? I
don't yet know what, but it should end. He who brings
something for many, won't want to bring anything to
anyone, he who gives nothing to everyone, may keep everything in the end, but only if it multiplied. Birth
control does not apply to money. I want it to stop, but
what is it, really, what do I think I see in money.
Whatever it is, I want only the gold, period, and then I
want others to stop wanting it. I do have to pay out, pay
the salary, because it doesn't pay when others hate me.
But there must not be any more hunting for the gold.
Because I will have spent it for the house and at the same
time kept it. They no longer have to bother. They bother
me in the acquisition of my wealth, which is the driving
motive for my directives, in all four directions. God.
And then I want to jump down on earth, I mean hump
Erda, so more earth comes about, for the dead to rest in
peace, guarded by you, my child. Earth, thrown over
the shoulder like salt one has spread around, so that no
catastrophe will occur. Well, she gave birth to you,
Mother Erda. So far, so good. So let's look at what she
produced! A human being is what she produced, well,
looky here, what an achievement!, hats off, she still
hasn't got enough!, even though millions and still more
millions are already resting in her, the dead; and the human still living creates a revolt so he can even say: I am
a human being! Me? I am a god, but even I revolt

sometimes. I am not human. Though right afterwards, the human being, the *Mensch* is dead too. Just because I said so. But the short time he lives, he sees freedom, for one moment, he sees it, just a moment!, he'll see it in a bit, he just has to turn a small cog, then he can see it, the fight for it is a work of destruction, nothing to be done about that, you've got to get through, through the work of revolution. Does this man go through with his revolt now or not? No, he doesn't. Jesus came close to it, he was sooo close to it. It wouldn't have taken much. We, however, have always been taken in, and by each other to boot, so where do we go, where do we come from, we go to the doctor when we take sick. Jesus just sacrificed himself as a whole. He negotiated with his disciples, he negotiated his price, but they could not come to an agreement and so he sacrificed himself, denied by all. And look what became of him! Now so many don't deny him any more. But now he is a god, that Jesus, by act of grace, but the grace he also had to deliver himself. It was not known before. He took the step, but every step a god takes leads only upwards. Not even you, child, make it, the revolution, in which I placed so many hopes. Uncle Herrmann and so many others, in whom no one placed any hopes, made it, the revolution. You, child, never will. God does not want it. I get you to sleep and you just do it, child! Just because I say it? You sleeping like the revolt someone had promised which, alas, never came, at least I don't remember who promised it, how many tried, but someone must have done so, a madman, no doubt, totally insane and I see it only with one eye, I see all of it with one eye only, but I see it coming, albeit not when, because with one eye you don't have spatial vision! What, I don't have a second one? Hey, I know that!, that's what I'm saying!, I am the first one to know it. And if you look at me, you know it too. The uncle of this woman also saw something, but now he sees nothing. I see eternity at least with one eye, that's better than nothing. Just because I will kiss you on both eyes, which will remain closed afterwards, just because I will guide you up a low mossy hill, with a wide-assed fir stretching over it? Just because I will remain lost in the sight of you, just because I will put the helmet on you and close it tightly under your chin? So that nothing will happen to you. That's what a father does. But he does it only once. Just because I will cover you with the long steel shield which is yours anyway? Did you never test, I am sure you won't be testing any more, if you've been awake all the time while you thought you were sleeping? Two eyes, are you sleeping? Because I said so, because I willed that the child, which I willed, will sleep? So now, a decision I made: now I want something altogether different, there still is a lot expected from you, that should flow from love and jealousy into universal human love. This is something entirely new and I want it now. I want to test it, I hope you join in. Too many people are already sleeping in the earth, for you, child, I could work out a different programme. You should do something, because nowhere would I be safe from you should you wake up, because I laid this on you, because I laid this drape of sleep over you. When you get up again, you are in for a surprise. And then we'll find a nice convent for you or an NGO, which takes care of those you'll have specialized in, and then, fine with me, we'll find the Aid for Africa, though Africa can't be helped, okay, so then we find Assistance for the Neediest, though no one's need can ever be met, then we find the Table for the Have-Nots, whose names are not recorded in any table, none would be big enough for it and, they are all registered, the names, I, a god, have got them in my head and those can't be helped either, not even with the miraculous multiplication of food, because they don't want bread, for a long time now they've also wanted spaghetti and fresh vegetables and fruit at the *Volksmarkt*, the people's, the popular populist market, because it is healthy. They get what's left over, like you. Unconsumed, a shelf-warmer, who won't sell out! Whining, always whining, but still lying there. That won't work either. They all lie there and eat what's left, but not you! You shall rise, child! Move! The hero is here, he's just parking his horse, oh no, he doesn't have one. He'll take yours, which you always took to the service. You will lend it to him. Jump around like the Pink Panther, you, the merry mare, yes, go ahead, jostle the stallion, have a ball! He can take it all right. Who's that on your saddle? And who hangs there, next to you, in the other saddle? I think those two don't get along and would kill each other again, if they weren't dead already. Be a *Schatz*, take these horses with the dead away from each other!, those two always saw each other only as foes. Set them far apart and bring in another animal, one that hasn't carried anyone yet, for such a one won't clean up its dead, it'll only take pictures of them, maybe our dear Pinkie?, how about that!, well, a panther, not so good, a beast of prey, even though a jolly one, the horses rear up, they are afraid, what seems to be the delay, you heroes, what takes you so long seaming your shrouds? They don't need seams and Germany also holds together without seams. That way it can grow bigger without feeling hemmed in. This panther and pink to boot! So funny! Kills people too. You know about that, you also know how! This Holy Germany, that once again has slept so long, let her bring forth people now, who go on with it right away, who bring it on! Offing is not that quickly forgotten! Such knowledge is passed on through generations. The legacy. It's gonna be a gas! That's all we needed. It must be done ten times at least, then that's done and the next ten and the next time get their turn. Unless the global fire comes between, unless the trailer fire comes between, unless the housing fire comes between. Unfortunately, something did come between, we are so sorry. Many are sorry who are rising now, after their almost one hundred year afternoon nap, it takes only one hour out of each day, but it also gives something!, it gives death, sleep is generous in this regard and they see, the murderers see, that the sun is somewhere else now and they can start all over with whatever it may be. There are so many volunteers, we can't even take them all. Or many more would die for Holy Germany. For the holy hoard. This Germany is a death land indeed, it is its journey, it is its trek, death, its journey is standstill, and making whole again what's been destroyed, now that at long last it is up and coming again. That others have it coming again. But this death, this tricky business Germany, this busybody Germany, its bodies don't stay underground, they look for buddies in the NS Underground, this death, which one?, *you* might, perhaps, find out, but only when I want to tell you, at least it made sense, if only for a few. They were carefully chosen, the victims, but the last moment, on a whim, completely different ones were taken. Whoever happened to be there. Gotta stay spontaneous, or else there'll be no one you'd come across any more. Gotta keep your eyes open. With so much death, one more or less won't stand out, not even ten, even hundreds would be noticed by us. So many are dying, after all! Some are dying all the time. It easily goes into the millions! What's ten people then? Nothing! That's the opportunity, Panther baby, take your pick! You are the final link! You are not the ring, you are not closing what's been open before, not even the front door, behind which cats allegedly are kept, but you at least are jolly and jump around the fire, some sort of cat yourself, you are so lively, limber and loopy, with your little two-step gait, yes, that's how you were thought up, that's how you took off, and you had to be taken the way you were and I like the way you are. The Norns' old lore, they know it, and what became of it? A funny pink figure, drawn, animated or also available as a plushy, for the child in us. So nice of them! That's how a work gets completed, if not perfected. With murder and a funny figure, that guarantees it's done properly, that this murder and that other one there are neatly performed to the end. The Germans are thorough, those free of property, unfree ones, but they are industrious, you've got to hand it to them, they go-get, they get rid of. Nothing's got to be handed to them and when they've finally got the Nothing, they promptly acquire it again. Always nothing, always the Nothing. If necessary, they invent it. Not the World Wanderer, not Mother Earth, not the Valkyrie, no, a funny panther it has to be. They learned humour in the meantime, the German heroes. Terrific. Godlike terrorific. A discrepancy occurred, don't know between what and whom. Something else happened. Something will happen which I won't understand any more. I will be gone by then. I won't have been at home for a long time before that. I will have wandered around. Something will fly into my eye, it's the wanderer's way, when he walks against the wind, I said that already. Always against the wind, until it turns into a storm. My house will be burnt. This trailer will be burnt. My colleagues and relatives will perish in the fire. Sadly, the insulation, which had separated the Germans from the rest of the world all this time will also be burned, because they finally learned to separate the garbage, the trash, as you would say, and they teach it to others. You, child, you will also burn and you will want it too. They all want it, they are dying to burn. We, the gods who we are to each other, who we are for each other – and today Valhalla is ours, and nothing tomorrow, nothing will be, because we, gods won't exist any more. It will be better. So. When humans get entangled in lies and contradictions like the State gets entangled, when they all want to be more than they are, we are superfluous. The Leviathan, the State in short sleeves, but with long arms, wants to set itself up for eternity, like us gods, and all of us are dead before we lived. We are completely out of it, we don't get it any more. Already now. I for one don't understand this thing with the Pink Panther. I've lost it, I didn't see the movie (or it's been too long since I saw it), I might have still understood it then, but I don't get what's become of the panther. It's beyond me. That those folks with their pistols want to get the State to collapse. I just don't get it. They could have relied on us, the gods. We can take care of it. After all, that's what we want too. Well, maybe not all of us, but I in any case want everything I built to collapse, I want to give up my works, I don't want to bring them along on my wanderings and when I'll be back home I want to go down with my works, that's what the Germans always wanted and so it will be done. Done deal. I want the end, only one more thing, and that is also: the end. And one more: the end. I can think of nothing else, the end means, after all, that nothing continues after it, but one thing still goes on and keeps going: the end, and after that once more: the end. But the end is not yet the end, before memory hasn't been extinguished as well. This will mean the real end. I see that memory has already been carefully deleted. Where we thought we saw something, there is emptiness. Someone must have touched the ring by mistake and now he can't let go of it. The trailer goes up in the air, the home aflame, the cats evacuated before, so that nothing happens to them, but the poor horse can jump into the fire. Cats saved, not the horse. The self-sacrifice has been decided, but they are still going to find the pistol, they will find more pistols and hardware after the sacrifice has been made, the self- immolation, the jump into the flames, the Valkyrie could have saved herself, you, child, could have been an exception, but you don't want to be and now all of us are dead. Greater are we in renouncing, than we ever were desiring murders, the dead. Ten people shot, but we are the greatest when we sacrifice ourselves, like Wotan, like me, so the self-sacrifice has been decided, greater in renouncing, yes, we announced it already and now we renounce our lives to go on. We renounce what we desire and that's always been life, but we brought death and now this is our end, let it be our end, we sacrifice ourselves like Wotan, like me, we don't have a child, for whom we sacrifice ourselves, okay, so let's just sacrifice ourselves, just like that, because we feel omnipotent now and capable to sacrifice ourselves. The will turns into the deed, which we executed ten times already, now against us, why should this be harder, okay, it is harder to sacrifice oneself than others. The fire. The end. We know no fear any more, neither are we prejudiced against the end, let it come, originally we refused it, if only for ourselves, not for others, we caused it for those, but now let's give a big hand to our end, please, end, come on in, you are welcome! No worry, no fear can fetter us now, no angst of death whatsoever. With the same passion we desired life before by taking those of others, ten people's lives in toto, we now take our own. Is there anyone who wants to go on living for us and in whom we can continue to live? More heroes? No volunteer? Then it'll be only for us, the end, and the Valkyrie may kindle and leave. Hostile we are to the stranger here, but he is still our favourite, because he may fall, felled by us. Sounds weird, but is true. Just like Wotan was totally hooked on the ring though we told him that this will be his end, self-destruction by wanting something. Okay, we'll walk into the flames now. We shoot ourselves, one the other, then the last one himself, and forward march into the flames. What remains? What remains for us? That funny figure, that Panther, he is the one coin too many that busts Uncle Dagobert's bin. Actually, he was a jewel, a real jewel once, something precious, his name he owes to a strange mark, a panther-shaped rune as I understood it. Thus he goes on living, unless he is set on fire. No matter. The sword's been forged, made by the hero. Only one or another knows how to do it, forging from iron filings and he does apply it, this skill. So, while you, child, are sleeping, that funny Panther frisks around the fire. To the end. That he doesn't get bored of it! No, he can stop it now. This is already the end. One ends oneself, or it's not really an end. Only such an end, one's own end, is one. You don't see him, but he is around, he is always around, until he has ended. He doesn't want to go on, he can't go on, he wants it and he gets it, the end. Where the thinkers reached a dead end, the animals begin to think and then even the artists get started. You don't even notice. He doesn't bother you, child. Nothing bothers you any more. Me neither, but I don't understand him. A plushy, a mere figure, and drawn to boot, drawn, as we are to death, drawn, like life, to destruction, a big draw, over-subscribed like a share, which is also available as a plushy, a fantasy figure, like the funny multiplication of money that topples everything that doesn't make it to the top. Ambition gets people there. They know how to get rid of people, the Teutons, who, however, will also end, like us, their gods, like everything, like the gods' gift in the *Führerbunker*, like his wife who didn't always want the same as he but got it, death, they all want to end, that's the end of them all, they learned it from us, after all, how to bring about the end. A lot of work but satisfactory to passing. Sufficient. All work burnt in the fire is past work. All work applied to killing is past work even before it starts. It's already been deployed ten times at least!, and used up. End of work. Full stop. And what remains? Objects. Nothing else. The treasure back in the Rhine, the *Schatzi* in her cell, all nice to each other or to one or more others during their lifetime, albeit not to us, albeit not to ten people, otherwise to many, maybe to all, nice, they still were there, they were there and now they have ended. All dead, which does not mean that they'd actually ended, but all dead now. What remains? Objects, rubble, rubbish. I can see no rhyme or reason in all this, here everything is rhymed, but I can't find a reasonable rhyme, let alone translation for it, too bad, really, all dead, all dead, the remains: autograph card Cindy of Marzahn, 3D-glasses, cat immunization card, coupon tooth-whitener, scarf with panther-, no, leopard-pattern, leather lace-boots, Microstar iron, red Santa hat, oversized, socks – red-white-blue-brown striped, ashtray with eight butts, almost burnt out, but not quite, Nintendo game, the book *1000 – The Best Baking Recipes*. All that could also be in other homes, by itself or with other stuff. Strange really, the things that survive fire! Perhaps too soon extinguished, the blaze, only the dwarfs still hammer on it, even though nothing lies there any more that could still be forged. All over. That's all that's left, all alone. Child, you too are all alone now. They all are dead, we all will end, in case they haven't done it yet, I will know that nothing is left, nothing of me, all my children, dead, but if I must go under, then the right way, then I don't want to leave my world to such people. But I don't even know now who those people actually are. My fault. I only know that I don't want to leave them anything. Forgive me, child, you had to go through a lot because I was so strict. You endured your father, you had to obey him. Now you may sleep. Take a rest, child! Sleep on the rock, keep sleeping, sleep, I am telling you, child! You do complain incessantly, as if you weren't my daughter: Papa doesn't love me, he never loved me, he always has to love something new!, and on and on it goes. Not the daughter, all the others, but not his own daughter! But love is not an end in itself. If you don't get it, you just don't have it. Someone else has got it then, or there is none at all. The cats were rescued, the men are dead and set ablaze by themselves. The few remaining things, worthless. No value, not valuable to anyone. Only the value itself is eternal. The value is mine. I am in charge of values, even if they come from someone else, even if they are forced on me by the wife, they still are and remain values. Many die for them. I, too, could die for them. The values are my children. My children also die and I die for them and because of them. All dead. All there is ends. Love the be-all, the end-all, but I betray even love. Only money is eternal. Money stays, just someone else has it. The money will stay with him forever or it won't. And so it goes. The circulation of capital is an end in itself which my love for all of you is not, even though all of you will be dead by then, only the money as capital is such an end, created innocently by dwarfs, later gigantic, capital, accumulated in a gigantic pile (pity, the giants can't see it any more!), which humans can no longer encircle, carry away, produce, spend again, waste, which humans can no longer hurt, for money is indestructible, for the valorization of the value exists only within this constantly renewed movement of the circulation, which simply, no, not simply, but still is: nature. Everything that is nature ends. But not this. It is the one and only that does not end, that never ends. We jump into the fire, others burn, we burn others in turn, but this never ends! Everything that becomes, dies, but not this. The trailer burns, the home is aflame, everything is engulfed in flames, but no one's fired up for us. Only one thing is alive. Something stirs and multiplies! It can't be us, but something's still moving here. The movement of capital is limitless indeed. It doesn't end. But you complain that Papa doesn't love you. Look at money, it doesn't have to be loved. The money comes from the capitalist and it returns to him again, always more than it was. He is the starting-point and the breast to which it returns, the money. Slurp! Even I, a god, am dead, typical, God died for you, but the money lives. Something's still alive here, thank God, oops, sorry, none is left whom we could thank. Only the money as *being*, as self, as be-all and end-all, as *I* is still there. The valorization of value, the objective content of its wanderings, like my wandering, earlier, when I was still able to, when I was still able to walk, when I still had my lovely lance, before an idiot broke it, those were the times! Okay, but the money wanders without it being able to walk, that is its purpose, and only the ever-increasing accumulation and the perpetual acquisition of wealth is the motif of its doings and my undoing. Look here, child, how nicely the money does it! Let it be your model! It never gets tired. It goes and it comes again, more than it was. But you whine, you want to sleep, must go to sleep, Papa wants it. You no longer circulate, have no currency, are not seen anywhere, that's why you are losing your value. The hero will forget you, because you don't move to become more, which means staying his. You really would have had to do something on your part for the hero to stay with you. But it doesn't matter. The gifted capitalist, not as a person, as such he is utterly uninteresting, but as personified capital endowed with will and consciousness. The gifted child is nothing compared to it. Not even the profit is something that counts. Not even the profit is important, nothing is important, only the restless gamble, the restless movement of winning, the restlessness, not that of wandering, but of becoming more. The capitalist becomes money. The owner becomes his beloved treasure. This passionate chase! Look, how your Papa does it: thus it is right, thus it is good. Should I exemplify it to you with the treasure? No, I won't use the treasure as an example, although I could, because the dumb giants and the stupid dwarfs and at least two hundred more persons who aren't even real persons, some are just creatures, some sort of beings, forest creatures, grabbing, snaring, that's all they can do, because all, no, not all, but some of them are chasing like crazy after this treasure. That's quite a story, I think; we could deal with it in our next newspackage, which will never be sent and therefore won't need any deals. My investment consultant keeps saying: No big deal. But it is. It's a huge deal. The capitalist, like the treasure-hoarder, I won't talk about the treasure-guard, though it seems to me there are more treasure guards here than treasure hoarders, but they all get killed, all dead, well, the treasure's still there, money, mind you, is eternal, it will survive us all, the only one to remain, that is, the capitalist, the only one left so that he can order the *Schatz* what to do – let's assume that he stays – strangely in the shape of three girls, funny twist of fate, women get it all and whoever remains takes all, everything belongs to them, three girls as the last capitalist, a holy triunity, no, perhaps a trinity, because they are never united!, it is, mind you, a female, that is, a disunity as God, as capitalist, that is, as that I was before, the capitalist as triad – now the capitalist is God, holy and threefold, like a paper plane or such, so then, this tireless chase after the exchange value, which it sets itself, what?, who?, well, it, which in this case was fixed by a shameless trinity who must stay underwater, until the treasure returns, until their *Schatz* returns, in the meantime he is in the war, beings falling by the dozens, the hundreds, and is kept for later, for the next war, readied for recycling by the god, it happens a lot, but only for heroes, the others must use the other toilet, a mass-restroom and, isn't that funny?, because: if giants, dwarfs, heroes, the accomplices of heroes, the accomplices and sisters of kings, the whole kit and caboodle, if they would not set the exchange value of the desired possession, it wouldn't have any. Neither would the treasure. It would be junk. A converted can, recycled paper, even paper money, with the signatures of the dead, which make it valid, a securitized bill of exchange, so that money can change the owner, but please, whatever it is, don't redeem it now!, a promise for later would make no sense, if it gets fulfilled right away, it wouldn't be a promise any more, this redemption should be neither claimed nor granted, only the money shall be there, no matter in what form, commodities also gladly accepted, which can go down the drain, if too many promises are made and, yes, this also applies to this promise, which will implode, if one spends the money, something like that, I didn't understand everything, but I know that something is very important in this: not everything at the same time! Not all at once. Not everyone at the same time demanding fulfilment of the promise stated on this paper, or *you* can wipe your ass with it; if I know anything, it is this: this bill is bull, it exists for show and it promises a hit and this bill is the playbill, it's a bill for a lot of bull that will hit the market, if the fans hit this shit all at once. Please!, one after the other, one thing after the other, yes, we speculate on everything collapsing when everyone wants to cash in on the promise, which this delay in the shape of this bill, this top billing of something one never gets, when this delusion suspends temporality, suspends time, and all this is accomplished by a bill to play with, with pictures and signatures on it, all of the long dead, because the pictures of still living folks are not taken, it would be impolite, because humans during their lifetime haven't yet achieved their final form, money has, it's right on the money, this top form money has reached, I assume money has now reached its final form, it cannot be improved, it promises everything and it keeps nothing, because it doesn't have to keep anything, no will, no way here, only a future in which it will be redeemed and thus people slowly but surely are themselves becoming the promises which are never kept, because they have learned that when a promise is really kept towards a real counter-value, which never exists, because this pile of paper can never be a beautiful car, this other heap can't possibly be a new washing machine!, those rags aren't even representatives of something and filthy to boot!, oh no, this call of the bank, these codes, these signs in the wires, they are not what one gets for them, they never are, they stand for it and they stand up for it, but what is it?, this cannot be!, oh yes, it can, it stands to reason, reason to be or not to – whatever, in any case, something must always be moved, these bills always postpone values until later, even though there is value to what one would get for them. But the paper is nothing, it just moves its owner into the future, people get postponed until later, just like their gains, for which they are working, everything gets moved, money is the least of all that gets moved, always later, it's always later than before, you always arrive later than when you took off, and people aren't even here any more, they were moved, those latter-day suckers, they promise something that is never kept, at least not by them, and so all people, like their measly promises, simply transferred into the future, and there they disappear, they don't buy any more, because they aren't here any more, they arrived in the future while still in the present, they cut to the chase, their bank.com for thousands of bills to play with and bought new home furnishings, in instalments, of course, they think they get things cheaper that way, but all they get is bills again, stating how much they already paid and how much they will still have to pay, plus interest, and people vanish completely in their promises of the future, when the products will finally belong to them, they hope for redemption, they hope that something will be redeemed, since they don't get anything at all for themselves any more, no one would give one measly penny for them, they want to shell out something, but this bill says that's not possible, because the bill does not belong to them, it denotes something, but that could be anybody, it could

belong to anybody, banknotes don't list names, nothing
verifies ownership, nothing specifies what is owned, no,
just the opposite, these little bull bills which buy you
something, which only indicate value, but aren't it themselves, delete people, including those in whose hands
they are, yes, those too, just the bills replace people with
something else which, of course, has to be something
other than a person or one might as well have just taken
the person. And this is how it is with the gold, the treasure, the *Schatz*, that can appear in any shape and
uniform, yes, also in that cave, with the worm sleeping
in front of it, fronting it, heaven forbid, that the gold can
ever get out, for then one could see how much it is and
even more play-dough would be printed, fine with me,
the gold can also appear in any other form, commodities
can do it, let the whole lot enter the scene, for all I care, I
have nothing against it, they may appear, perhaps not all
at once, and not in the form of money, if you please,
kindly in another form!, they can't all be on the money,
they must not be on to the promised bull on the play-
dough bills, all people cannot be and only when all of us
are toast, will it be redeemed, the promise, this funny
money, this phony piece of paper, no idea if it burns as
well as our single-family detached house, there is a lot of
stuff and insulationf in it, that makes paper so lazy and
that's why it can endure so much, paper is patient, you
know that, child, since you are a hobby writer, and of so-
called plays to boot, who can never properly end a
sentence, right here, for example, I've been looking for
the end for quite some time; this is why I even mention
paper, this paper here, and what appears on it, whatever
it means, but also paper in general, *Schein*, paper, bills of
meanness, appearances of means, *Schein* is paper parlay-
ing the value noted on it, that postpones redeeming it,

always into the future, always later, this redemption and that other, holy one, always happen later, it is a promise, but don't *you* expect that it will actually be redeemed!, that is, *you* can claim it, but nothing will be redeemed, it could spell doom, but the boom must go on till it busts, so then it may start all over again and so it goes, and that goes for you too, child, don't claim anything from that paper, and yet it denotes a treasure, a *Schatz* indeed, something that fills a hollow space, guarded by a worm, which is what everyone knows how it feels, who ever had a bank account, that is, de facto everyone, everyone can believe in the promise, everyone can believe in this treasure, which he is made to believe exists, that it is already here, been there before him, that treasure, that's correct, but it is the Nothing, the treasure, a nothing, maybe not exactly the Nothing, though in any case nothing, but the participants in this hunt are, so to speak, the shapers of this treasure, they made it, because they could agree on its value, but it was their value, we don't get anything out of it: Value – very high! Anyone can dash that off. As paper it is nothing, paper is patient, as we say, when it gets written on it, the value, when it is named exactly as much as it is told, but worth nothing. A promise that's worth nothing. And yet: the highest that exists at the moment in the whole world. You can't get any more than that at the moment. The interest rates are lousy, if one stays normal. Normally, at this time they are always measly, and that is why one has to do something with the money. And it grows! We are dead, but the money still keeps growing! We can no longer water golden apples, but the money still becomes more and more! Help! We can't stop it. Soon there will be something higher than anything imaginable and that will be the money, higher even than our mighty fortress, it might be the Dollar or the Euro, the Renbimbi or whatever it's called, no idea, but we'll be dead, the gods will be gone, only the money, the *Geld*, the gold, will be left. What did I want to say I haven't yet said? There isn't anything I haven't said yet, thanks for the applause, I know you want me to finally stop, but I don't want to, I don't want to, because at this time I have not lifted the treasure, well, yeah, I did, once, long ago, and I gave it away, I paid, but I did not lift it, I can't acknowledge anything above me, only the sun and the moon and the dear little stars, but nothing else. That is why I did not try lifting the treasure, it would be above me like a big star. I will die and someone else will lift it and have it, after I will have given it away, the trinity of the three daughters will host it then. The original own-ers will get it. Always the same will get it, the *Schatz*, because they always had it. Only the in-between, beati-fying love, will be gone then, yes, and life too. The money stays. Hello, money, you stick around now! But in the meantime, it will have wandered, the treasure, the *Schatz*, what meaning would it have had otherwise, what would be its purpose? All of them, giants, dwarfs, gods, heroes, humans, yes, my pleasure, women too, goddess-es, fine with me, they sure did a number on me and they all reached an agreement, and that took hundreds of years, no wonder that giants and dwarfs want to come to an agreement, when even gods manage it, but with the others it just takes time, we also want to have a common understanding with animals, we help it along where we can, there is the sign to the stockyards, follow the mark-ings!, they lead directly to the arrivals hall!, if, well, yes, if this succeeds, it would be a project of the century, but they finally did agree, the exchange value of the treasure is set herewith and with immediate effect sets genera-tions in motion, they are all very moved, the treasure hoarders had their success and thus the crazy capitalist merges with this treasure hoarder and they become one, no idea who that was, but I know that this one was pretty rational, after all, he knows what he wants and he's got it, clean deal, but the capitalist detaches himself from it, he detaches himself from the mother ship, the treasure, the hoard and drifts, to the sounds of waltzes, into outer space, so then, the lifeline will be clipped straight away, all the waste, the filth, will be dumped into the vastness. Caution! The restless multiplication of the treasure, the increase in the exchange value, driven by the sullen hoarder himself, the rational hoard-horde-shaper, now drives what drives him, he drives the machine himself, that sullen *Schatz*-educator, because besides his *Schatz*, his student, he sees nothing, he doesn't see the market rates, he learns nothing, but he accumulates, he's got his stupid *Schatz*, okay, its value has been established, I know, I know, child, you've also got your *Schatz*, but where is he now?, where did he go?, he's got another woman, someone's got to tell you, even your *Schatz* has another one, but not this treasure hoarder, the accumulator, who has current spritzing from his fingers, that's how wired he is, I mean, from the strong current, he tries to save money from circulating, got it?, he wants to save it, he wants to keep it, he wants to guard it, he wants to hire people, animals, ghosts to keep it, stupid like Italian sea captains, he wants to keep it. But modern Anthropos, the capitalist, the modern capitalist, doesn't want to keep it, he gives it away, that is his sacrifice, he does not jump into flames, he circulates it all over again, it's like a compulsion, for who knows if it'll ever return to him again, you, child, also believe that your hero will come back to you again, but he'll do that only over his dead body, he's got another woman, even the capitalist sacrifices his money to circulation and waits patiently, that it – having become more and more, ever more – will return to him. Got it, child? You are waiting for your hero, but he won't come back, he has forgotten you, albeit because of a nasty trick by other capitalist pigs. Whatever. But the capitalist per se, he's got my utmost respect, my admiration, all credit to him! Just sending the money away again. Risking everything! That's greatness, let me tell you! Now I could enumerate all those creatures along the Rhine, who are called *Anrainer*, a silly pun on Rhine dead in translation, so let's just call them rhinos who simply want to keep and guard the treasure, it probably would take a whole day, all those names, awful, not even a god can remember them all, well, I couldn't do it, listing all of them; so, let me tell you: smarter are those who give away the treasure, who throw it away so that it come back as *Mehr*, that is More, who throw them into the *Meer*, the sea, where this pun drowns, whereto the net profit, the Rhine's wet, but well-washed profit flows. Fill in here, you do it too, child, the names of those who ridicule the treasure, who throw it away just for the purpose to let it increase or disappear, as the case may be, unfortunately I am not on this list, that's quite a risk one would have to run, I'm not running it, I'm just running out, like all the gods, who want to retain their power, instead of just throwing it away, everything coming into being, comes to an end, yes, all that is, anyway, humans disappear, I hear screaming, wailing, the gnashing of teeth I don't hear, but otherwise everything, they reach for something that's leaving, to also circulate, like everything else, that's right on the money, the *Schatz* is right, it stays with no one, only the one who dares something, it just depends what. A hero won't make it, he won't make anything, he will die, he will perish like us! Only those are right who scoff at it and give it away, the treasure, their *Schatz* so that it either multiplies or disappears, one has to risk something, I said it already, I don't belong to those, I did not want to belong to the losers and now I am the biggest one of all. The simple circulation of rings, necklaces, bracelets, all that junk, the yellow scrap iron people buy and sell, because they think that's the only way to maintain value and possibly get more for it, since they also obtained it themselves, idiots, not very entertaining, anyway, this circulation presents only the exchange, buying and selling, purchase of gold and jewellery, wholesale and retail, always buying, always selling, people are lined up to the streetcorner because they have to sell off their family jewellery, so they can keep their family, what did I want to say, nothing should be kept, not the jewellery, not the hoard, not the ring and not the family – or have you seen me recently with my family in the new fortress, child? You did not see me, doesn't matter, it would have been too late anyway, there was nothing to iron out any more, not even with the new iron that was found in the burnt house of the new heroes – I am with you, child, now I am all yours but only briefly, I keep wandering and then I return home, and then it's all over, then we all explode, but I won't let myself be squeezed among that stupid bunch I call family, the wife and then the sister-in-law with her golden apples, there won't be more of those, the apples don't multiply, but at least they don't vanish either, and youth can be replaced by a good plastic surgeon, one still must die, yes, even if one is a god, and why not let him be old, what did I want to say, okay, so the value of the horde, I mean, the value of the hoard, is guarded, by many, they all want to have it, they jump at each other's throat for it, they kill each other, who cares, in essence nothing happens. Nothing changes. The treasure is always left, the only one, and if it could laugh, it would. But when you throw the money away, when you stake it, when you circulate it, when you give it free rein, let it loose, then, well then, suddenly both function, the money and what one can buy for it, commodity and money, both, clawed into each other, from the beginning, they love each other!, it certainly looks as if the promise, substantiated by nothing, secured by nothing would finally come true, but it only looks like it, it will never come closer to its delivery, the promise, it isn't close enough to the future they hope for, but they have none, only a god can deliver this promise, that's easily said, but even I, a god, can't do it, it is a religious promise, the promise of a god, the proof of a god, but not even a god can guarantee, that all that stuff will still be worth in the future what fits as a figure on a piece of paper: Fricka and her new, single-family home, which, however, is real estate, an immobile property, not a mobile, bad example, but you know what I mean, commodity and money and commodity, commodity and that with which one buys it, neither works, well yes, they do work, that's what I am trying to say, they only work as different modes of existence of value, depending on who measures it, who measures it with what and for whom doesn't matter, it doesn't matter, only the standard must not be forgotten, so that it can be applied, no matter to what, commodity and money: two existences, two fraught existences, who know nothing about themselves but will get to know each other soon enough, oh sure, they still can make good, they still can make out, commodities and money as two modes of existence, sounds like talking in code?, well, that's German thinkers for you, as essences, *Wesen*, as existential essences of value, of value itself, with money its general, the commodity its specific one, as junk, so to speak, as something useless, which, even so, is highly desired, even by the very top, as *Dreck*, and *Dreck* as disguise for modes of existence of one and the same thing! And both morph incessantly and without a break from one form into the other and vice versa, they change the shape, they change the clothes, they change the light bulb, the *Birne* that is, and this is not an ethnic joke, for Germans the *Birne* also means pear, the fruit, as well as the head and what's in it. In short, they also change minds. The needs for owning them change more or less, the one wants this, the other that, they all want possession, they all want the gold, it serves to secure their safe, their treasure, but the securing branches out on its own again, no matter what's written on this piece of paper, some have only gold, gold keeps its value, right?, those dumbshits, those lunatics, do they really believe that at least gold is the mostest and keeps its value, which these numbers here, on the screen, these mere numbers express, represent or whatever. Gold should deign to represent value, and the value is supposed to be fixed to boot? Stay fixed ASAP? Gold becoming computable, predictable? With paper? Baloney! It's got to go, it must go, like your father, the money's got to go now, everything must always wander, only the gold lies still while it wanders, I'd love to know the trick, reducing while lying around, no sport, no beyond the comfort zone, no movement, the gold lies still, rests still and heavy like the lake in the old German *Lied*, doing nothing, it doesn't vanish, but it won't become more either, no, it does become more, but it could also vanish, whatever. Capital is money, capital is commodity, capital is both, inasmuch as it can separate from its owner. The solution, the final solution is the dissolution, no, hold it, not yet, is the separation, is the emergency solution, is steady change which can't be had without separation. OMG! And so on. No matter what, you won't get it, because you will sleep deeply and won't circulate and won't hunt and do nothing but sleep. The hunting, the hurried, the hurrying hero gets something, I just don't know what, except that he will get death, like everyone. The hero. Before that he'll put on an unbelievable show. Some hero, he, a hero is he who is identical with himself. And this form he would only have in the form of money, for then he could not die. He could ride, run, sail, fly a kite, but he could not die. But your hero, he's made a mistake, I think, right from the start. You'll find out soon enough. Without taking on the commodity form the hero does not become a hero. Without taking on the commodity form, the money does not become capital. Without taking on the hero form the hero hasn't got a chance with you and he won't get one either. Without the money acting militantly, as hero against the commodity, as in the hoarding of the treasure, which caused us so much pain and *tsuris*, without the hero and the money fighting, if not always against each other, without the money being let loose in order to confront the commodity, money is stupid on its own, it doesn't know that it needs the commodity, because without the commodity it is nothing, it despises the commodity, money does, while it is dependent on it, what did I want to say, a treasure will only come to be, when the money gets hoarded. But we only get to be capitalists, when we reconcile the money with the commodity again, finally reconcile them again, not as heroes, but as dealers, who, on the other hand, are despised. Dealers are always despised. Armageddon-ish consequences, luckily not in my army. Okay. Now I am talking as a god, who will soon wander, like money, without anyone being able to run rings around him, the capitalist knows that all commodities, as shoddy and schlocky and cheap as they may look (they all find their takers, that's for sure, whatever *Dreck*, someone will buy it, and sell the copy of it, only cheaper, count on it!, someone will find it, who will think he's made a find, even if it's the wrong one!), however much the product might stink, a god now dares a comparison, listen, child, however filthy and smelly the commodity might be, nothing works without it, the money is nothing without it, it belongs at the table, it is part of it, it sits with us, it sitteth among us and hath dwelt among us, like the word, the word itself: the commodity, the commodity itself, in person, even if it's ugly, small, puny, stinky, it is part of us, we are inseparably bound to it, it is our family, the commodity, and families are also different, like commodities, the happy like the unhappy ones, baloney, families supposed to be different!, it sitteth to the right hand of God, no, not mine, another god's, there it sits, the commodity and with his left he pays it, no, not I, I don't pay, another god, a saviour, that's not me. A saviour – the ultimate prophet, who counts his profits. His money is worth nothing without it, the commodity, and commodity is EVERYTHING, it dawns on him at the latest, when his sister-in-law is to hand over the golden apples, this precious, priceless, but much praised commodity, and hand herself over to boot, because only she knows the right fertilizer, then, yes then, even a god will catch on, that contracts are stupid, because you never know who is going to win, what did I want to say, so the capitalist knows, that all these commodities, these wares, this waste, this rubbish, the rubbish even of rubbish is, in faith and in truth, money, that commodities are internally circumcised, listen, child, a god knows what he says and he says it here, because he can, because no one can prevent me from doing so, and who would that be anyway?, I say, all money is nothing without the commodity and the commodity is nothing but a circumpruned Jew, incomplete, but always efficient, always efficient, this is what I foresee, until he also ends, oh, I don't know, I say that, a god, and the commodity is what counts, a miracle, the miraculous multiplication of everything, not just bread and fish, and Jesus, well, a blockhead too, and that's a no-brainer, there is no free lunch, Jesus gave it all for nothing, but he was a fool, believing that this would get him something, it would get him followers, really now, I don't see them, not yet, what did I want to say: so then, the commodity is the miracle worker that must wander in order to make money out of money – which must wander for a specific purpose, namely this one or nothing can be bought for it, because the commodities are often nowhere near the money, which must wander in order to make more money out of money, to make more of itself. To make more money out of money and off and over. No, not over. This too will no longer be the case at some point. Because the money itself will take off, without commodity form to make more out of itself, so then it will make more of itself, money on its own will be able to do that, it will no longer need the products, you'll see! It will have cut itself off from the commodity, which once was so dear to it and helped it so much. But a god does not forestall himself, he creates. But he does not forestall himself. That's pie in the sky as we say. Better than in the face. The Germans put it more romantically: 'That is music of the future,' to which I say, without the music. That is the future. Money won't need the commodity any more, it will be able to do everything itself and independently, for which it still needs humans right now. Money will become free, free also of humans. It will be the only thing left. I already said this. There will only be money, I just ask myself where, but the money will know, it will be right there, after all. All of us will end, we will be dead, but the money will live. Long live the money! Maybe a hero will get it, the commodity, the bride, whom he desires sight unseen, since she is still around, the hero is still looking for her right now, but he knows she is there, since he knows that she is on hand, handily at hand for him, soon, the commodity, which commodity?, the commodity! You? The hero's commodity? It is you he desires? You he loves? You, you are nothing without the gold, you count only together, right?, no?, only you two together count for something to the hero, to make money out of money, which the money can handle later all on its own, even without money, without being with itself. You are already off the handle, because you counted on the hero. The pure hero doesn't care about money, why should he care about you, the commodity he is looking for? Why you of all people? Because you are sleeping? Any woman can do that! No hero will come for that. No hero comes to just any woman, a hero comes to none, but to you he will come! Do you know why, you little lovebug? In love with the wealthy father earlier, now with the hero, whom you don't even know yet, whom you have never seen? Only that he's been destined for you. No idea what's his name, but he is destined for you. Are you sure? Yes, you know this for sure. I know it, of course, for I did the destining and I already knew then: this hero will be just a stint. What if he is the wrong hero, that is, not a hero capable of a relationship or suited for a relationship? Not fit for a relationship, but maybe for more relationshopping, and shipping and swapping? Or only ready for a relationship with another woman? Yes, and it's the same with money. It is exchangeable. But only a few have the opportunity to exchange it among each other. Though this way it increases evermore. With you, my child, it will be evermore, you are an unbeatable team. The hero scorns money, but he is looking for you, the fulfilment of his desires, behind the fire. You know him by his scorn for money? You are crazy! You would also be nothing, were you not my daughter. I am the surplus value, I bestow on you, you, a living, if sleeping substance, thus the hero will enter into a private union so to speak, with you, which in truth will be a union with himself, a private union, but still. It will be valid, if not for long. This hero will always only look for himself, because ultimately, he only wants to have a union with himself and no one else. And those coming after him will only watch speechlessly, how the money itself enters into such an intimate union with itself, how it wanders autonomously, like a god, like a hero, like an animal, moving freely and autonomously out into the world, this is how it'll be, believe me, in the end the money will stand all alone as the one and only holy lone ranger and wooer, as the only free citizen of itself in its golden empire, where the sun never sleeps, but never rises either, because there is nothing to rise to, no prices to rise without any other commodities, nothing pays off, the hero's calling doesn't pay, because the money can't collect itself. That's what really rouses him, and in the end the money, as the sole citizen of its empire will also enter a relationship solely with itself. O sole mio! Everything else will be gone. Only the money will be there. What do we need the guilt for, the debt? Because the money is there, which we, for the sake of our debts, must pay back. But some day the money will do everything all by itself, it will even run into its own debts and be able to pay them back with itself. It won't have to pay anything back, because it sets its own value and that is always measured against itself. So then the money determines its own value, because humans will be far away, gone, dead, extinct. And then, only then, it won't need the commodity any more. It will be free, the money. It will also be free of itself and thus only then be itself, wholly itself, its holy self. The money will be liberated, it will have this private union with itself, which is no one else's business, it is private, because no one gets the opportunity to own it, it will wheel and deal and seal the deal, solely with itself, one money with the other, as a primordial value that differentiates itself from itself, but neither will know how and why, it will become the God-Father of itself, the God's Son also of somebody and both, money and money are of the same stock, the same age, both will lie on the same altar, money and money, where they will sacrifice themselves for themselves and still become more, by sacrificing themselves, no more debt and no more guilt, not gods, not heroes, not daughters any more, from no one, no interest any more or only such that the money can agree on with itself, money for money, for money money, more money, always still more, that's the goal. No one to fault. No defaults. It will never be sufficient unto itself. No money will not be an issue, because the money will not go for it, the gods will go for going for good. Money however will never make that mistake. It will only go for more!, yes, the good old money and it will be the most restless wanderer, it will wander, travel incessantly through the world, swirl round the world, for its own sake, your father, with his stick and his hat, child, will be *Dreck* compared to it and from *Dreck* it will come as well, the money, just that it will be more durable than any god. No one will know himself any more, no one will know his neighbours, his relatives, only money will know other money, by its money money will know itself, by its money you shall know it, knowing means not touching, only looking at it and recognizing it. Multiplying and simply being there, as More. We will be the quiet observers of the money and its fights, and God-Father and God's Son form one person, and this one person, God-Son will sacrifice himself once again, for himself, not for the people, for himself, sacrifice only for oneself brings the money, because only the surplus value of the sacrifice will turn money into capital, it devours everything, it also incorporates all the bodies it sees or uses, that which was *Dreck* once, is everything now, because it will have turned into everything. *Dreck.* And as soon as money became capital and as soon as the Son and, through the Son the Father were produced, no, not the Father through the Son, though, mind you, that is also possible, it will also be possible then that even procreation turns itself around, yes, birth too, everything in reverse, nothing in verse, no rhyme or reason, only capital, only money, which will have to have multiplied, something like that, then time will begin anew and also interest computations and compound interest computations, which I didn't understand the first time, will start anew, at zero, there it will also stop, finally!, and thus, as soon as the money's relationship with itself will have kicked in, as soon as all humans will have kicked the bucket, I already said that, the commodity relations will disappear and the true relations step out of the shadow, money please take over, yes, with pleasure, I take over, I am the only auto-mobile substance, yea, nothing has to be computed any more, the god must wander, I, however, the money, am the only auto-activating substance, it has its ways, it hikes on its own, it hikes itself, the money, it knows how it ticks, a substance, into which everything flows that ever existed and which flows into everything that has ever been thought or taught and has ever been produced, commodity and money, that wonderful commodity I've been talking about so much, well, yeah, sadly, it will be gone then, too, it will have become money, by then the money will have totally forgotten that it would never have got to be something without the commodity, the money will have forgotten its loyal stirrup holder and everything else, it will have forgotten its purpose, since it can do it itself, since nothing else will exist any more, commodity and money, both mere forms, if pretty or ugly, who could tell, mere forms, easy to move, something flows in, something flows out, there is no more, there is just money. For its own sake and for itself. Me too, a god who made himself the lord, but only because he was already the master, I myself will also have turned into money, allowed to wander endlessly, incessantly, ever-evermore, if no longer in the shape of a god, of course. The value the value the value is the more and more and more, the *Mehrwert, the 'more-value',* in the unmentionable's language, because it had to become more and more, added and added ad infinitum, or else it dies, or everything dies, falls, withers. What have we got here, what's going on here? The Son produced the Father, who on his part will have produced him earlier, an endless chain and if the Father was produced through the Son, the difference between the two disappears, every difference disappears, there is only one thing , which we already named several times, I hope *you* remembered. There is only the one, unfortunately there

is always only one of it. One of one. Primal production
by one and not by Ur-mother Earth. Money by money.
Everything flowed in there, i.e. it flowed into this little
can, which once was another can, which turned into
another and then again another one, sometimes even
two cans are made of one, I was that can, something
flowed in there, the differences vanished, waned, for you
can no longer tell that the can had once been another,
maybe even two cans. And it's all one and the same. And
they both are one. And the Father and the Son are one.
Well, the Spirit disappeared, and the mind got lost in its
wake, but who needs it anyway?! If you do need it, you
surely could use one. The money goes adrift, it flows, it
lets itself go again, it gets a good run for itself, then it
runs out again, any way it wants. It's good for the circulation, running. And the circulation is there, so that
everything always starts anew again, over and over
again, but it always has only the same things at its disposal, which, however, not everyone can have, not
everyone has the right of disposal, it is called divine dis-
pensation that not everyone's got it, that not everyone
can have everything, good, all clear, so far, and again
and again it starts all over again, and that's how it is that
it is and does not end and then it does end nonetheless
and all over it is. For good. Well, well, so the child, my
daughter turns away from me, with all her hopeless
fondness for a hero, who will also be gone soon, the man
just leaves. Doesn't go to where the genital – the hole or
whatever it's got there, the child – already took on the
leading part. Goes elsewhere, no, money doesn't interest
him. He fears something else, which to us is totally
harmless: cut and run from sex! It can be so pleasant,
though it can also get quite unfriendly, but it won't
count any more, it won't mean anything any more. The

dynasty and its secret life won't mean anything either any more. Simply cuts and runs, yes, your father too, goes away and leaves you, child. Finds the exit and goes. The genital, that's what it used to be called when there was not yet a hole there, where the woman is, now everything is a hole, so the daughter's genius sinks, she gets sort of pulled inwards, I think, the daughter's interest, however, can't be directed inwards, she sees nothing there without a mirror and torch, it can't get active there, it needs something or someone, better someone who shows her the Nothing, the end, that is, where there is nothing and where the Father lost his right. Where life came from and where there is nothing now, is where it ends. First the child wants life and then it must want its end again, as the Father wished. In the meantime, there is a lot of careful ruling to do, more even towards the end, because people as a rule react in panic. Work must be done under conditions most favourable to the accumulation of pleasure so that the child's dependence on its sex becomes more bearable. While the male child keeps plenty busy manually with his hydraulic sex-lever, which can even be driven in and out – everything money can do itself without anyone taking it in hand – so then, meanwhile the daughter, unrewarding, unrelenting, vanishes inside herself. Money too has vanished, also in itself. It is no longer graspable, it is the only thing still there, but no longer within grasp, because no one will go for it, there's no one there to go for it. It is graspable for no one but itself, the money. Anybody at home? Nobody at home. The house was burnt, the trailer too. Yes, that too. The newest murderers will have gone with bikes and city maps to the sites of crime and also returned from them again, GPS they won't use, even though they are so new, those heroes.

But they don't want anything new for themselves, only the solid old. *Dreck, Dreck, Dreck*! I know. You too, come to us, give your best! Never will we be reachable at a contact address or number, though this doesn't mean that we are unreachable. Comrade! Enemy of the German people! *Sieg!* We aren't talking about you! You, take your lives! Take the lives of others! You are entitled to it. Take it! Take these lives now! Ride your racy, raceproof bikes to where you can take the lives of others and afterwards your own! Now! You accomplished what no one else ever accomplished, quite a hit, ten years of murdering, that's quite an achievement in a time when achievement usually doesn't count any more, only money. It is an achievement, we celebrate the tenth murder anniversary with the Pink Panther, Paulchen, as we tenderly call him here, he is our guest of honour, but maybe our understanding of honour is different from *yours* or his. We will expand the dominion of our killings, there is nothing *you* can do about it, even if you had anything against it, we execute the deed and what flows back to us from it as satisfaction, pride, joy, we can add as extra capital to our life, yes, that's what they say or something like that; the extra product flows already towards us, the dead, dead heroes, women (well, at least one) who carry them, which they add to the Great Army of the Killed, until the trailer explodes, from where the heroes on their bikes start out and where they return to again. This is exactly how they imagined it, those heroes and this is exactly how it gets done, they ride in twos, they ride on two-wheelers, albeit not into the woods to rest and graze!, no, they still have a job to do, those warriors, who've got their strife, though not against each other, only the foreigners, only those are foreign to them, the heroes' hatred won't settle down, Paulchen the panther,

114

the pink one, would be more likely to do so than that hatred, we are still waiting for the heroes right now, Holy Deutschland would give us a grim-hearted greeting, were she to see us approach without the tenth victim on our teetering iron steeds: the Valkyries as bikes this time!, not on, *as*! As bicycle messengerettes with, like, heroes on them, not bad either, heroes are carried around in the saddle, heroes who, we hope will rise again and continue to fight when they recover, but no, they prefer to kill themselves then. That is the golden chain, which the wage labourer forged for himself just like the killer, which everyone forges who does something, or puts an end to it, the golden chain, the treasure, the hoard, the slumbering depot in the Rhine! We add ourselves to it, it's pretty loose, the golden chain, but it can be tightened any time. A loose chain on the murder-cycle, that's not going to work at all. Those are also human beings, someone says, but personally I don't believe it. People, different ones. Different people. People, sadly already different. I liked them better when they were all alike. Especially under one roof. Most of all my roof. And I also liked topping-out parties. Only with our house, the giants, in their hurry to get the gold, skipped it. No, no topping-out-Fest skipped by us. It doesn't cost anything, except labour, and nothing costing anything any more doesn't cost us, after all.

B: Must I really be gone from here, must I bid farewell to you, never go to bed with you, I mean, go to bat for you, Father? Obeying someone I don't know? Throwing myself on someone, anyone, and if everyone were a hero it would make no difference, you always ascribed this to me, and because you thought I was so hot for this, you ascribed this fate to me. Pushing myself on someone who doesn't want me? Since the hero always wants something other than what he's got at the moment. He wants to lead the eternally creating life, but he dies anyway. He wants death to be where he is not, but then he still rather dies himself. The hero always wants to do everything on his own, he wants nothing that exists to perish, even if he has to take care of it himself. He wants everything to perish and he takes care of that too. He wants, he wants, he wants. The hero goes down. He goes down with all that exists. The hero hunts, he hunts persistently and single-mindedly, but in the end, it is he who has been hunted. The hero wants to destroy the dominance of one over the other, the power of the mighty, so that he alone is powerful. But he will perish. He will die. This hero won't give a damn about power, he won't even know it, this is why he'll have to die, die as an insult to all the other power-mongers with their bummed, their pumped-up power, even though the horror of this thought almost floors him, that's where he will end anyway. He will try to break the power of property and the violence of the powerful, but he himself will be broken, because unconsciously, not unconscientiously, he is part of it. He will want to recover the treasure, as the only one, but they dumped it into the water, because before that generations of heroes slayed each other for the treasure, hundreds slain, thousands drowned. Just for the money. Just for the money? Just for the money! They dumped the treasure into the water, so that no one would get it. A rational attitude. Centuries of war for the gold, but now this is the end of it. The gold is in the river, all is in flux, the river doesn't yield, so the hero must step up to the plate, but luckily not into the water, so that at least something happens. The hero is the killer-deputy, the *Führer*-deputy, the deputy of a deputy, all the way to the top, to God, who appoints the deputy and then kills him, because he always must remain the one and only. There is room for only one. The hero, a deputy of God, an angel, and the Father must be hostile to him. While actually the hero would have to be his most beloved. Thank you that you leave him to me, Father. But in the long run no one can keep a hero. Earlier, heroes killed each other for the gold. Now only the hero gets killed. The hero stands for everything that one is not, but must be offed. He is one too many. What one can't achieve oneself, what, nonetheless, must not even exist, must be off. Instead of striving oneself unceasingly. And this is what I should want? His own will the hero's master? Better than the average Joe – absolutely! I'd like to meet this guy, is all I can say. In any case he'll be better than average, before he will fall, thank you, Father, that I don't have to take just anyone, only the one no one is looking for, but who will put an end to you. Tier three: the Helpers. Mediocre investigators find only mediocrity, no question. But the heroes are different. These three here: one the intellectual, the other the terrifier, Loge and Hagen?, no, no way!, no enlargement from this negative!, that's not how it is done today. On the hard drive we are all the same size, unless we enlarge ourselves. This woman, the heroes' Frau was dealt with quite neatly, bathmat and curtains are something we heroes do need, the woman? Yes, this female Jesus-softcover edition with her 'I am whom you seek', Gutrune rather than Brünnhilde. Gentler. Gentler than I at any rate. Gutrune is the one who cooks, who cooks for the heroes, while I at least am on fire for them, but still sleeping at this time. And yet it will be a go. But it won't go well. They won't go out, the heroes, so that they won't be seen. And we certainly won't run out of them. There!, new ones are approaching already. We already got hold of two. Two pieces plus half a Valkyrie. There they hang in the saddles, partly dead, the half of the Valkyrie is still half alive. Who hangs there? Obediently we name the names of the heroes. Take your brown guys away from the horror, no, that's not how it goes, pace Richard, I know: '*Führt eure Braunen fort von dem Grauen*' 'Take your bay well away from my grey', I mean, the one horse away from the other, come on, move it! You, dear grey, will now be led away from the bay; now you, dear neo-brown shirts, you won't be led away from the nightmare you have dreamed about for so long! On the contrary. You are pushing forwards into the fire. You take yourselves there. You bristle in your bridles. The stallion jostles the mare. We can't allow this. The world turns around. The warriors' feud turns even the horses against each other! The world turns again. Calm down, brownie, don't break the peace! But that's what heroes love to do, they love it most! Dear Brown Shirt and dear Grewsome in Grey! A warm welcome back to you two. They regrow, those heroes, as if they could gain strength from the soil. They do, indeed. The holy ground does it. As long as it isn't too steep, since they will bike. They will go on vacation, be nice and go camping. They will drive the trailer to the campgrounds. They will be polite to the neighbours. They will buy a round, they will be normal, they will look athletic, they will have been outside in any weather. They will always come back home to their trailer or to their nice apartment. They will all be like everyone else or like no one. Or they'll stay home altogether, where it is most beautiful. Like me. No, I don't mean I am the most beautiful, only that I stay at home. Sleeping in the rain, in the sunshine, in the wind, in snow. No, not sleeping. Biking. Always biking, the hobby of the heroes. No, not

118

all heroes, but of those. In the den a loft bed, a guest sleeps there, who is not me. My eyes have been shut by a god. Those heroes' ovens get cleaned by the wives, the neighbours get a plate of brownies, I am not among them. Brownies from a recipe in the cookbook is not my thing. I can't be in any book. I can't be at all. Why is one part of the apartment *verboten* to strangers? Why is everything *verboten* to strangers? Why on earth did they forbid everything to strangers? Here only for heroes. Heroes: please leave yourself here. Hang yourself. No, that wouldn't be the right exit. If there is no more room on the coat rack, then just leave it! Heroes, please leave your lives here. His own pleasure the hero's only law, his own strength the hero's entire property? The highest about the hero his productive killerpower? That makes the hero? Once a hero, always a hero? The hero as the only free human, with curtains, tiles and doormat? He also needs that sort of stuff. The hero staged? The hero who steps out as a model, but can't be one? The hero as producer? As begetter of new heroes? No, the hero as hazmat, as terminator. The hero as the only one alive amidst the products of the lifeless, the weak, the powerless. The hero as destroyer of order? The hero as liberator of the slaves, of the few?, the hero as his own master?, but those few as heroes of themselves? Well, there's no one else around, they don't leave over anyone, those few as the slaves of their own power? When will they catch on to it? That they turn themselves into slaves, into slaves of themselves? Just because they decided it this way? No, they didn't intend it that way. Definitely not! Rising labour costs – but our labour power is not for sale! Real slaves can mutiny. Their strength, together, the power of those who are not heroes and don't own bathmats or the matching toilet-seat cover, their goalless power, the power of slaves – those are folks who don't want to make something of themselves, while the heroes want to always be on the make and so they are – their power gets sold again and again and sold again and resold, the power given away, gifted as extra capital, giving oneself and that's no small thing, since even curtains and bathmats must be bought and one has to toil like a slave for those things. The heroes also have all this. It falls into their lap, they don't have to work extra hard to keep anything, they don't work, they don't sow, they don't reap, they are not fed by a Father, yet they get fed. The work gets delivered, *you* know by whom, but one part of it always remains unpaid, so why not *not* work at all and be a hero instead, maybe not instead, but in general?, now, that takes some nerve, calm down, will you!, I just wanted to say: it takes some nerve, but that's not all it takes to forge a sword, some heavy duty stuff is needed for that, actually it's chippings you need, small pieces, you see. I can see it already, that's the last thing *you* could bear: several pieces like this. But I, I say sooth: labour *über alles*! But where to put it? Someone will take it, with gloomy contracts and tough laws, you do need those. The dwarfs need them. They want them. Question: would the State accept the option of love as a means of payment? No, love cannot be accepted as a means of payment. Especially not for taxes. Now, who actually does pay for this *Schatz* right here? Well, not that putz. The customs officer, no, he doesn't pay, but this time we are not dealing with a hard up, no, not hard on, he's got other needs, okay, so this time we are not dealing with an impotent, an incompetent officer, who guards this embattled borderline, it's about money after all, not life and death, and this officer inquires twice, who pays and, most of all: with what? We have no money, we have no cash on us, there isn't any in our SUV, none in the purse of my en voguely looking companion that could even vaguely, let alone vaginally interest the State. There is nothing. The State has no claim to the coat with fur collar, the new watch, the shoes, in this case Jimmy Choo. They will never belong to him, he can fret and frisk us all he wants. Whatever he finds, belongs to us too and not to the State. No, we don't have money on us, what for, anyway? And if we had any, it would belong to us alone. And can we please drive on, the lady has to urgently use the toilet and I think that the State does not levy the tithe for this, the service area does, if only for itself, now that would be something! a toilet-tax! Really, no cash?, says the officer. Well, then get out of the car. But we don't want to get out. But you must! Move it! And what's this? What's this? Seventy loose Hunduns, *not* Huns, they don't come up in our *Lied*, our lot, no kidding? No kidding. Seventy hundreds, just in the shirt breast pocket, and where they come from, there are more! And what's in the purse of the lady, who needed the john so urgently before? Seek and you shall find. There, in the side pocket we find a whopping eighty more of those bills. Might you have pawned the Nibelungs' treasure? Traded it in for paper? Devalued? The value creation of thousands of dwarfs snuffed out? This beautiful treasure which harbours so many desirabilities, which is blamed for so many murders, even though it never killed anyone and just laid there quietly, now and then playing cards with the worm, that was all, did you turn this fine, this fabled fabulous treasure into paper, which you carry illegally? Where does all this paper come from? It must be the outcome of a much bloodier crime, that you hid it so well. Did you slay somebody for it? Shame on you! But we don't understand: such a tremendous treasure and now only those few rags? Sure, it's not everything, but still a shame! It was pure gold before. Why did you do this to the gold! But all those Hunnis, no, not honeys, the hundreds come from Germany, inspector, sir, you can see that this is only paper, who would exchange a treasure for paper?, and besides: the worm could have watched more carefully, he bears part of the blame, all of this is from Germany and goes right back there, we just take it for a short trip across the borderline to Liechtenstein, the 'bright stone' state, so to speak, above the tree line, but those are slippery slopes not everyone can get across, only a hero can do it, in this case a hero and his wife, they can do it, they conquer the border with a few kilos of paper which once was a treasure and still is for the one who's got it. We only wanted to buy some jewellery abroad, no more, no less, rather more, to complement the *Schatz* we've got at home, a few pieces which are not in the treasure, but absolutely go with it, and in any case, we need them urgently. But we didn't find anything beautiful, therefore we bring back the money made of paper, we are honest, we are honest finders, and what we found, we actually forgot. Consider that the hero also had to first look for the treasure! We've already got it, but we forgot it in the meantime. As a matter of fact, we also deserve a finder's fee, since we found the treasure and now we just can't remember where. What we do know is that it belongs to us. God, are we happy, that it is here again, albeit in paper! At most, this could be a misdemeanour, gulp! We forgot that we turned part of a treasure into paper and smuggled it across the border, please forgive us one more time and don't convict us, you, man of the border, it really borders on civil rights violations searching people so thoroughly! One can't even bring paper unnoticed into other countries, without attracting attention. For the whole treasure we'd have needed a few trucks and they would have certainly attracted attention. So we very much restrained ourselves. The truth wants to come out briefly, it is already at the door but changes its mind and walks back inside again. The worm also checks who came. Some items of the treasure are missing, but otherwise everything is hunky-dory. Where is the worm? Does he have something to do with this Herr and Frau Gibich from the Rhineland wanting to bring the treasure cast in stacks of paper, of bills, across the border? The dwarf notices and forgoes love on the spot. He sees how easy it is to get away with crime and chooses the path of sublimation, he replaces love with money. Done. Love: something with much too much ado about it. Sublimation is if you get little for much, if you replace much with little. That's no big deal. Anyone can do that. Thousands of dwarfs' hands toil, forge, hammer, grind, file and then drill a hole into it, whatever it is. But this year they have to do without the Christmas bonus and convert it into labour, sublimate it in labour. They don't mind, since the top dwarf also denies himself something, he denies himself love. His people would never do that, they sublimate something else. Better, a cold, uncomfortable living room, but the TV still works, the marshal can't march off with that. So the top dwarf, a dark elf – what an ass he made of himself – definitely does without love. No problem. He'll never get anything for it, but give it all instead. If he had known that! He would have loved to love. If one would ever know this before! Now he's got nothing. He is permanently divested of everything, which others will divert in turn, for example this well-heeled couple from the Rhineland like he, the dwarf, fellow Rhinos!, how nice!, though taller and a twosome, because they did not deny their loved ones back home, they are already waiting for the money, what did I want to say, it depends on the stage we are in now and currently we are in the stage of denial, if not for long, we hope. It's only a dwarf, after all, who practises self-denial. He does without and takes the surplus value instead. He takes everything, he takes over, now the dwarf takes over, who earlier denied himself love. Now he wants to deny himself even more. Dwarfs aren't usually heroes, as we know. And the other dwarfs under this hyperventilator? What can they do? Those guys work. They labour. Does the hero liberate them from it? Does the hero liberate everyone? The Rhinelandish couple liberate themselves. So it can't be so hard. Well, we can forget them, no one can accomplish this. They will be notified, Herr and Frau Gibich, she is a stupid cow, he I don't know what he is, they will be reported, because they failed to report their money when they were asked about it twice. And before the cock crowed a third time, they denied their poor money. They wanted to spare their money, was their excuse. Because of constant changes the poor money has gone through enough. So, in fact it could never adjust itself to anything concrete. The hero also goes through a few things before he forgets me. The Rhineland – a *Reich* of forgetting! Meanwhile the hero liberates the gold from the water and re-establishes the cycle of killing? What on earth is he thinking? The hero as sport for speculators and money makers? Hero anyway. Here my summary, Father, begetter, betraitor, hero: I know, it could be done shorter, but not with me. Writing can always be shorter, but not speaking and not me either. And in writing I renounce shortness as well. And all this for me? I can keep it all for real? Sleep?

124

Fire? Revenge? Smoke? Disappearance? What the dwarfs don't get, who, after all, must labour constantly, I can take? All this you destined for me? The hero too, please! Add the hero on to me!, lay the hero with me, please. The hero as the One and on the other half the rest, that the ground welters and waves as if it were the Rhine carrying the treasure? Let me tell *you*, he's got it in him, that Father Rhine, he's got no beams, unfortunately, water never does, it swallows incredible amounts, no matter what. The sucking water. It swallows everything. Until people, howling and screaming, wrecked ships after a disaster, fly away downwards, no longer held by gravity. No uplift to buoy them up. The buoyancy in a fluid equals the weight of the replaced amount of fluid. Too many on one side. Only one on the other. As if that could be so easily calculated with liquids! The revolution? The opposite of entropy? The rising up and standing out in this uniformity, this uniform Wagalaweia, this Here and Now, this one and the same, that gets all the samer everyday, but never produces equilibrium? And by that I understand something different from physicists, who all will die too. All of us will die, yes, me too, you maybe not, Father, but then again, I think you too, my sister just told me frightful things about you. If the hero were the revolution, he isn't, but it would be nice, he would eternally make it in life, while the god makes eternal life, an honest-to-God con-fest, I mean, contest between them, a horn-call will ring out, everyone will straighten up and look where it comes from, all will rise and turn slowly and reelingly around their own axis, no horse picking them up, where actually is east? Now everybody stand up for me, please, the hero, who always says please and thank you, will ask the guests. And then he will say, after everyone stood up, now sit down again. That then will be power. That's really nice, someone having power and not abusing it! He'll show it to them all right, the hero.This will be his power, people standing up and sitting down for him again, this makes him different from the plant, when a seed is planted in the ground, it stays down there and that's that, only people, the roly-poly dolls, can always bounce back up again, in that old German TV show they even have to, the signature rings out, the horn call resounds, the hero enters and commends the people to his will. Well, he commands the people that his will be done. A god. At least like a god, comes quite close to a god, really, you can judge that, Father. How close he gets to you. In divine rapture they jump onto the stage when the hero calls them up one by one, no, that guy he doesn't want, he wants the lady there, yes, her, in the hall of heroes, albeit only as the groundlings in that hall, come up to me, please, so that we can do something together, dear fellow men, don't deny each other any value!, for: verily I say to you and I show you this lady whom I'm calling, now she actually comes up to me on the stage, how happy she is, look at her, she can hardly walk from all that happiness!, I chose her, I picked her out of the audience and then I will tell her what she has to do. If, as the chosen one, you want to make any statements – I am no longer interested! I am already ahead of you! I am beyond you. So there she is, who slept until now, or worked, what do I know! People jump up in divine rapture, maybe next time the blond hero will call one of you, you never know!, a groundling will be called, seed material will be sunk into the ground, come on now, sink it!, sink!, it will be done one way or the other, it must be, the audience member, led by the hero will have to say, *Ich bin ein Mensch*, I am a human. Something the hero is not, of course, but he wants others to see how that would be, being the others, or being like the others. And *you* are seeing it now. The hero shows *you* on someone substitutionarily, a she he chose himself, personally, from the audience, how this lady here falls from the high horse on which she came, directly onto the stage, with a harrowing howl, something like this, no idea how that sounds now, approximately like that, I am Waltraud and I come from Königswusterhausen, that's very close to here, I can explain it more precisely if you like. Not necessary, it's a place with an unpronounceable name and therefore could translate into anything. But what goes for all those places: don't ever go there!, go elsewhere and be someone else!, please!, listen rationally to what I tell you! Since we parted from these places, we are no longer sent to battle by our fathers, for our fathers have learned! My name is Waltraud, and I am here to pick up the dead heroes, to scrape them from the roads, pull them from under concrete walls, lift them in their cars out of rivers. We have so many mid-range heroes, that's what most of them actually are, crazed and clueless, riding around on their machines or in their tuned-up or low-rider woehicles, an *angst*less army, in the meantime absolutely fearfree, yep, that's right! The fearless avoiding their fathers, because those were still afraid. They were scared shitless. These here are already the new heroes. We can use them up and they use themselves up quite eagerly too. We can let them jump over running cars into their own end, they can break at their necks or right in the middle, in our midst. Okay, the audience is now led to the world-ash, but they don't want to go there, they only want to watch, because they would have to fell the world-ash, that's a lot of work, our guests could also do something that's not so dangerous, where they can't get killed by falling trees, they could also break their legs together, that's better, because they could still sit afterwards, maybe even stand with crutches, they could get damaged some other way, our hall guests, not the hall daughters, not the Rhine daughters, no, the guests, the dear guests here in the hall. The audience stares fixedly at the heroes enthroned on their high chairs, I mean high seats, yes, all of us are also here!, here as there: only heroes!, everybody wave *'winkewinke'*!, yes, and now there comes this harrowing, shattering call, which I still owe you, Frau Waltraud had to practise it first, but here we go now, she screams, she screams, because the hero Father ordered it, she screams, she was chosen, after all, because she can scream the loudest and most shattering: *Ich bin ein Mensch!* Oh my, no one believes her. But we certainly can come up with some other human! And that one throws himself to the other millions, who unfortunately could not get a place in the hall, but are sitting out there at their devices keeping watch, if not *The Watch at the Rhine*, because that had been foolishly entrusted to three clueless girls, no, hold it, only to one, namely this one: wrong piece, how could I've been so off the mark, sorry, but there are so many women, they can get easily mixed up, so then the entire treasure and only three girls to watch over it, who don't always have time either, because they have to practise for their next synchronized swimming show, sorry, digression, and stupid as well, like everything by me, thank you, baloney, looney, nincomboobies, topless, clueless as so often, doesn't land, too much dumped into it, that's why it doesn't work and here, what's going on here on stage doesn't quite fly, director, can you please see to it, that all lights are turned to here now, otherwise I digress even more, please, all you've got thrown on Frau Waltraud from

128

Königswusterhausen, wherever that is, the lady was chosen speficially by our hero Father, so now she knows her lines, she memorized them earlier in case she gets chosen, wanna bet they worked that out beforehand?, and she screams, *Ich bin ein Mensch* and she falls, and millions of people at home at their devices, where they sit, quiet and serious like gods and the chips of the screens, which they crushed in a rage, no worries, they are quiet now, so then fists clenched tightly around the chips until they bleed; those millions won't come back again from their TV seats and they won't be carried back either, those heroes of the everyday. Doesn't matter. They stay were they are. No blood flows later, when they gawk into their smartphones or tablets, I've got one myself, the hero too, of course, he though, by the by, hasn't got you, Father, you've been replaced long ago, by a device, that can do anything, although it did not create itself, the device, that wonderfilled device, it was also conceived by a man, meanwhile also departed as a hero, unfortunately dead, who never did anything but selling absolutely special things, making them famous, forever young, even though dead in the meantime, deceased, yes, he too, it just might be the prototype of God-Father's will, did you mean that, might you have meant him, Father?, that hero was the embodiment of the Father, every father whose children hunger for music devices and thirst for telephones, did you make that man, the lonely man on stage, yes him in the black rollneck, no, not the one in the rollator, he's nothing and is never meant, no, the man there in the cone of light, the spotlight, holding such a device, yes, exactly that one, the very latest, did you mean him when you wanted to create heroes, when you created heroes as a prototype of your will, when you wanted this device, which you couldn't even imagine, even if you

129

would have studied at the university, Father, God, did you make him an idol, a hero, THE hero who was to awaken me? Not really sure, Papa, if you got it wrong, maybe you meant another one after all? That one, sadly, went kaput. So, maybe yet another one, he – another? Think, Father, think hard, if one of your offspring wasn't more fearless than this one, more foe to you than this one? For the hero is always foe of the Father, yes, also long-time foe of the wireless telephone, already way back then when we were not really living yet, a foe, why not, even though we, we took it to be *le dernier cri*, compared to which Frau Waltraud's crying out is nothing, speaking without wire altogether, that's it!, a horrible *cri*, but it liberated people from a wire that chained them, that's something anyway! It was magnificent. The hero as the Father's foe, the new as foe to the old, the hero as foe of my old man, patience, my boy! If you think I am old, you should show me respect, me and my old Notebook, which still works quite well, I swear, in Africa ten people at least can still poison themselves later with the e-waste and I, I don't need a new one yet! May I still keep it for a little while? No, I may not. It's gotta go! The sons, while knowing nothing, easily know how to help themselves. It's gotta go! Everything's gotta go until there's nothing left, no more stuff to blow our mind, and we won't know what hit us. Because our last eye might have also been blown out. For that?, no, not for it, maybe because of it?, no, not for that either, but in any case, it is absolutely certain, that the Father will be replaced – Frau Waltraud told me earlier, in private, in the checkroom, while she was grasping my knees and I remained blind to her pleading glances, by the hero the Father shall be replaced – even though, I don't know, the end of the world is upon us, the clouds close in, vapours

rise, flames flicker all around me, you think this man
with the razor-sharp device (lo and behold, it is a knife!
He's always got a knife!) in his hand will be able to ensure the rebirth of the world? That man with the device
which he must now hold into the light for the cameras, a
device as image, an image of a device he holds in his
hand, do you think that man, or rather his device solo
could be the will to become the world? Could be, I am
skeptical, Father. Before I fall asleep, I ask you to consider: the recently deceased, the first-rate hero candidate,
he didn't invent things, he didn't think up things, he
didn't produce things, he couldn't even imagine something regular – I mean something that obeys regulations
– let alone these things, they first had to be shown and
explained to him, but he represents something, but only
with this thing, with this little lighting device (no, it's not
a light-bulb, that would be too big for him), alone he is
nothing, but the simple, pure hero is everything alone,
this device carrier's job is to exhibit his thing, to represent these things here, he himself has already turned
himself into his thing, that's because he can't let himself
be represented by anyone, therefore he has to represent
himself as his thing, and here, look, here he holds himself up to us, holds himself before him, that little thing
that exists independently of him, it's not grown on him,
because it is the thing-in-itself. For all this he is put on
stage all alone, with, no, in a black turtleneck, so that
only his face is seen, nothing must distract from this face
except the one he shows, only his face and this device
that shines in the light, a device with which one can do
anything, even things one would never envision, are vi-
sualized here, the goals are set, just that the flight height
does not, as in tennis, get set in the regulations and the
range has always been limited by net and lines, but now

it isn't, the range is almost infinite now. A hero for sure, this man, who presents devices, a representative, but a representative of devices, standing behind him are only these devices, no one else stands there, surely a hero, but THE hero? He who was supposed to come? No, rather one who has to go. I dare to doubt that this one will wake me up, I mean, he is already dead, he couldn't stay the course for long afterwards, they wouldn't be heroes if they lasted extra long. Okay, so he could sell the things he is showing here, he couldn't make them, he couldn't think them up either, but he could certainly market and sell those devices, no matter where, that was enough, and now this hero who did not hesitate to put himself in pawn, fell, fell over like every hero, albeit not fallen in the field of honour, fallen, not live on our show, he got felled, like the world-ash, he fell over, just fell over, Frau Waltraud will tell us live about it or she might not, and all of us, who were frozen in fear, return now as good customers. This hero has fallen, I admit, I already admitted it before, but this hero remains dead, he stays dead when he is dead, the hero doesn't. So far, all dead, and the woman on stage screamed earlier: I am a human being! Yes, that's what Frau Waltraud screamed, you all heard it. But she'll die too! So there! She didn't say, I am a heroine, she wasn't allowed to, actually her only job is the transport of heroes, no, she said, a *Mensch*, she threw such a fit, because nothing else fit her description either, sorry, but she said it because the hero told her so, he ordered her, and then there was this '*Ich bin ein Mensch*' scream into the mike and now they all crash, the millions, the living revolution, God turned human being, no the human being turned God, no, at least the God-willed human?, no, this can't be it at all, God wouldn't have wanted this and besides, you are it, Father, the god, you can appear in many, but this one you would not pick, you would never appear as a Frau Waltraud from Königswusterhausen, you might send her to us, as your messenger, through silent rows she would steal away and come to us, but you would never choose her shape, I know you well enough, Father, and that man in the roll-neck, that's not you either and you wouldn't want to see me in that role either, you intended me rather as a role model, but for whom?, no other woman is suited for it, uhm, so then something will be announced, but I am no longer listening, the millions at the TV screens use the break which is brought to them to woo them, to go to the john, the screen stays in the meantime, people don't even see how much they are wooed on the bright shining screen with all that shiny sham, they can't take it to the loo with them, no, and not to the grave either, but other devices for sure, you can take them with *you*, the smaller the device the easier to bring it wherever you want, a brightness like a creator's emanates from these people, no, not from these people directly, but from these newest devices, which are flatter than pieces of paper (so why am I still writing?!) as if each one had its own creator, it's quite wondrous, a totally new human appears on the screen, yes, also on that one, very small, you said it, these screens are also available in very small, as of right now you can always carry them around with you, you can look into them everywhere, anywhere you are, soon also through your own glasses, yes, even through the ones you read with, that is, you'd actually want to look close up, rather than far away, no matter where, a brand new human in his shining light, even if it is a sham, with which we have no experience yet, but it's the same sham anyway, only the device is new, so then, fake, no, new, therefore right, this is the sentence which, at the same time is its contradiction, do *you* recognize this sentence? Yes, you even recognize the brand of this sentence which, as I mentioned before, is based on experience; if I could think, if I'd I know what I am talking about here, I don't like it, but there is one, it can't be said any shorter, and this is also a sentence: there is one whom I can't describe in one brief sentence, because he IS this sentence, I have no experience, none whatsoever, which I could express with this sentence, I don't need the sentence, but I do need this person on the screen, he means something to me, but I can't say it, because I have no sentence for him. I can see him, but I can't say anything about him, the hero, the proposition and contradiction in one, some see him, the few who don't need to, the others, who are in the john right now, sorry, they don't see him and this new human, made of mud and equipped exactly with this shiny mud-head, the mud-*Birne* which already came up here before somehow, he can't do even a hundredth of what his devices can do, his body will soon be finished, because he can't control it, only the remote control, only the fingers, he's still got those, he still can move them, with which he swipes across the glass, or whatever it is, yes, just like that, and now he announces to the world, well what? Well, let's say the new gospel of happiness. It could also be something else, but I take that one. Because I have no sentence for it, you can also call it something else. I don't care. The ones who see him, have it, the device, the smartie, because they listened to him and swiped and did what he said, the others don't, too bad. My dear folks, it is time, a time has come now, no idea which, it is a time, in which, no, whatever will be, it won't be peace and quiet, that's a fact, nothing is fact, except this, dear folks, don't deny each other your value! The hero has his, but you have yours too. The hero has more value, you less, but you don't have none!, for nicely you stick onto the bags with the merchandise value the sticky label, so practical, so then you put your value onto the thing in the bag, only the new coat is in there, I know, you did not make it, but you put a value on it, which is written on a small tag, that's also labour, producing this, writing something on the tag, you are telling me!, if anyone knows what it means to write, it's me, but anyway: producing anything is labour, the value presents labour, it doesn't do it very well, I think, this value is not a talented actor, I rather take the commodity, that is, the device and don't do the work which nonetheless flowed in there somehow, the way big crowds flow, at the Love Parade or wherever, where they trample each other to death. Everything flows, people flow about and crush each other in beat with the music, I, unfortunately, don't beat around the bush, that's why I am writing this: therefore keep writing!, don't ever stop!, the people also keep moving after all, but music is music, it turns you on, there are so many who want to hear it, ideally together with others, listening to music with other people, could anything be more beautiful?, there are so many among, no, under them, under their sneakers which get lost when they stomp on each other or strangulate each other some other way, the shoestrings don't hold together, because the people flow along so fast, so many of them, everything flows, the music too, completely unhindered, if someone tried to hinder it – now that would cause some panic! When they can't hear anything, people get really angry. What to do? What do we do with the driven ones, those driven to the stage, they head in droves up to the stage, that's where the music plays, what do we do now that they lost their shoes, where are they to go? What they are up to and what they are into, is obvious. Music. They are no heroes, mind you, some could become one in this exceptional situation, not to be confused with expected situation, if there are exceptional situations, you can also expect exceptional people, but they are not excepted, okay, they are excepted by the promoter, but they are not excepted from the collapse, from suffocation?, what is emerging here?, a vacuum? What's building up inside the hero?, inside the man who's holding up this little girl so that she can breathe, he did not make her, but he still holds her up so she can make it through the chaos, that little darling, what emerges here but not among most of those who are trampling others to death?, the *Mensch* emerging here is not he or it what I understand by a hero? He is it or he isn't. No, it's the other one! No, that one's not either. The labour that's invested in something, must also get the chance to express itself somehow and it expresses itself now, just like Frau Waltraud or whatever her name is, the labour expresses itself now and runs down over the people's ears. The hero chose it, the little girl chose life, she determined to breathe and this lady here chose a new coat, into which flowed the labour of human beings who often are still children, I said it already, flowed like the Rhine, just small-scale, that's what I am saying! I won't digress any more, Papa, because it's about the two of us. My hero won't even look at the gold, he will get it for others, but he won't have any interest in it. He will be interested only in himself, the self-born, the self-made, the self-mate. He doesn't need a hero, the Father, the God doesn't need anyone either. But he has everything he needs, because he created it himself. Let only one rule: The Father! The All-Father, that is the Father of all, the uni-creator, yes, also of the universe, God Father, the glorious! Only He. You. Father! Though I don't know who that hero is, I'll bring him to you, I'll bring you the hero, please be nice to him. Be kind. He is the guarantor of your eternal power, Father. Though it does not need guarantors, but if it needs one, it'll take him. Good thing, he'll have been murdered! That will make him easier to transport. He will be your bondman but, in this case, after me. I will bond with his body, then you'll get him. At least once the daughter comes before you, Father! I know, this is not how you imagined it, but you don't always win either. The heroes succumb to you, everything succumbs to you, of course this hero too, no question. He won't look at the money long enough to realize that the gold, the money, also represents a human relation to production, but he won't be interested in this relation, only in himself, the hero, like you, Father, but you can afford it, you made yourself, but the hero was made, you had his father killed, even though he would have never been competition to you, not he!, but, just to make sure; the hero was already in a womb, in the womb of a woman, hard to believe that a hero can come out of a woman, not much ever comes out of one, but enjoy this new warrior! You approached a well, and there the Norns' rope was hooked up somewhere, the Norns are also listed somewhere where we don't find them and you pulled at the rope and you pulled out a bucket of water, no, you pulled out *The* buck, *The One and Only*, others are working with the rope of destiny, also women, you are approaching their well, because you always have to approach women wherever you see some, there you go, your only eye approaches the well, though he himself is the spring, the hero, but he can't see it so well with the one eye, the Father, yes, you!, Father! Pardon me, but he doesn't see spacially, it doesn't matter, since everything he sees he made, he knows what it is already before he sees it, he listens to what the women hanging on the other end of the golden rope will tell him, what do they tell him? In fear they see the gods who rule by betrayal, they betrayed even two giants, they would betray them all, but none is left, yes, those giants, first they still were two, two little giants, then the betrayal and then there was only one who, for security reasons laid himself on top of the *Schatz*, so that he can sleep on it occasionally, no hero he, yes, to the unfree they seem mighty, the gods, yes, but not to the free. Somehow they don't. And only a god will know, and he will also say so, that one human is greater than he and he does not have to be a hero, well, in this case he is one, but he must be free, well, I've never seen a free human being and therefore not a freer one either, but if he is free – and I don't mean free as in available, he is more than a god, mind you, I never saw such a one and never will either, but he will be more than a god and he will defy the gods and if he fights for the gods, he will do it voluntarily, at least he will think it is voluntarily, okay, maybe he will be interested in nature, that alone sets him apart from the crowd, except for fans of nature and natural cosmetics, maybe he will understand the little woodbird, he will understand the language of animals, he will also understand the TV moderator, my ultimate hero, which is no big deal, fine with me, he will understand everything, but he won't look at the specific social qualities, despite his high standing he won't be able to see the qualities of an issue, this issue, these qualities, he won't see it in the social qualities and qualifiers and he won't be able to make a sentence out of them, because he won't know what he is talking about, he won't be able to tell that all of them, all those qualities and qualifiers, many of them having become masterless, have turned into money, he'll be the only one not interested in money, which everything turned into, he will deal with it rather playfully, it won't be handed to him to increase it, he won't get his hands on it, so it can't run through his fingers, he will have belonged to the oldest *Volk* in the world, despite all that, the Germans, who fortunately own the hoard, the money, the treasure, which everyone wants to get from this *Volk*. This *Volk* comes directly from God's son, it still is totally out of breath, now it is God himself as well, it sits on its hoard, which is a *Horst*, a lair, when the German will have become an animal, he sits on the hoard, a hero, a glorious hero, from whom all other peoples come and immediately want to get something from him. *Der Deutsche* dishes out. Mind you, he can also take, but mostly he dishes. He must be able to take, but having to dish out we taught him. An *Erlkönig* will not suffer death for the sake of salvation. He will be the oldest king over all peoples on earth, the German, the "Alder-king" who still has his temporary licence plate, he has not yet been approved for public traffic. I speak this sentence as proof: only a few can be kings, because they might suffer death at it. Some don't even want it. But everyone wants something from them. Luckily, for all peoples, the world belongs to the Germans, verily I say to you, even if it is not true. And now we all want their money, all want the Germans' money, the hoard of the Nibelosers, it was always by a hair they did not save us. Maybe they must save us this time, maybe they won't escape our supplications, not be able to refuse us, those kings of alders and willows, kings of everything that is pliable and also bows at the right time when the right one comes to them. The Wanderer, the Germans' wander-god, no, this time it isn't the money, this time it really is their god, he is the only god, Wotan, the wanderer, who did not have to yield to the Saviour, he became the Saviour. The hero, also the Saviour. How many actually are there of those? They are all related to each other, that's why they are so strong, even if they don't appear together. The Germans invented the only hero who becomes *the* Saviour and furthermore, in crucial points similar, very similar to Jesus, the Son of God, likewise the hero, the Son of God, who was gentleness incarnate, Son of God: Love, but the hero wants and is another kind of love, which he desires and which he becomes. He must die, he will be murdered and will be avenged and then finally justice will come about. The door will slam shut, the Germans will all be locked up, their hoard will stay or rather be returned to all who want it, to all it belonged to and were robbed of it. The Germans have it now, in case *you* have questions, in case *you* still have questions, ask the Germans, learn their language, that's the first thing, ask them, if they will finally pay, since they have to anyway, as Christ is the Father of all humans and the hero made us, the Father, Jesus becomes Father, God, the Father who made him and now Christ produces us all in series, after all, he knows now how that works and we just wait that we can shit all over him. The Germans pay. Period. What says the bride, what says Gutrune, yes, that's her name, don't blame me, it's what she's called, but she doesn't count, she's just some bride, she is not me, I am the spiritual bride, what says the woman, the little woman, the cutie, who would not rent part of her home to foreigners, she can't become the bride of the hero, because she is already the bride of two heroes, deceased in the meantime, burnt, blown up at least partly, what says the poor bride, all alone now, heroless, the heroes' lot was not granted to her, she still had to take care of the cats, they have no business in the trailer, take the cats to

140

the neighbour, she had to do that, so that they won't burn. There she runs, the bride, all around town, the trailer blown up, the apartment set on fire, the cats dropped off at the neighbour before, basically a good person, all of them good people, unfortunately also murderers, no, not the cats, what is she saying?, she says, the maiden, she says, this poor bride of a pitiful brood of dwarfs, who took themselves for giants, she says, the German bride says, and for that she has to make a special trip to the pigs!, well, *ja*, she does have to do this in person, she says: I am whom you seek. She says the words of Jesus. I already said it, but I find it super cool. And then she never says anything again. Then she says nothing. She says these words to the police, but no more. She was not searched for, but she says she is searched for, she first has to convince the police that she is she and the one they are searching for to boot, she does not say that to the mounted police, she says nothing, she denies nothing and gets jailed, because she is the one who is not searched for. They would have never even known whom they were searching for and on their own they would have never found her, they found her cute, her home too, with its runners spread out for the one who is to come, that much they knew, but they did not know when and who that is. But the mounted, like the unmounted and the unminded anyway, who now, though, are mindful of seeking advice, they definitely made up their mind to do that, all those officials, and this is really official!, would have never found her, if she would not have come on her own, a female Jesus, well, some deviation from him, Jesus's bride, beatific Beate, not bad either. Beate Zschäpe, look her up, she is the one whom they seek, and she will be stopped right away. We won't need a fire around her. Nature will be restored to order again, I

141

promise, it will be soon!, though *you* won't understand the little woodbird or any animal, no animal that will be murdered and screams and is afraid and eaten, at least a few pieces of it, *you* won't understand any animal, that *you* won't understand the woodbird either doesn't matter either. And the Germans will have to pay. This sentence is a fact. I can say it. They don't want to, but they must. There is nothing more to say because I said it already in this sentence. That's too simple to be said? No, nothing is too simple for me, I can assure *you*! Now on we go: he can see her nature in nature, the hero, the god, yes, but also her distress, he can see that too. As to the gold, which only he doesn't want, we certainly do, he only wants to save us, though we don't even want to be saved, in gold he sees nothing, even though it definitely looks like something. That the process of saving would be much easier with the proceeds from gold, he doesn't believe, the hero, he sees nothing in it, he wants to get it for others, but he won't want any of it for himself. He will know he wouldn't have been able to keep any of it. Well, he could have, he would have been able, but it doesn't interest him. He will get it for others, but he would not want it for himself. And now to us, Father: you must want me, Father. You are not the only one who must, the hero also must. So that already makes two! Plus all of nature, which we poor humans never learn to read. The fire will be enough, no one will be enough for me, but the fire will do, you only have to set it, Father, then I can read it. Nobody gets through it. Only one gets through. Others might be allowed to want me, heroes may, unconditionally, the one hero, Jesus, always may, but you, Father, you must know – I've no idea – in which discipline the hero will compete, but it will be a discipline in which he will compete all by himself. He won't

142

have an opponent in this discipline, that is, after all, why he chose it and that is also why he chose me, because through the fire he won't have any opponents. The trailer will have burned, the apartment will have burned as well, the cats will have been saved and not roasted, the maiden will be in jail, but that doesn't interest the hero, he knows that as the strongest he will win, no opponent would dare to challenge him. Until he will die the hero's death. That is why he decided, what he will win against whom and afterwards there will be the feast of horse plus hero plus wife, in the fire, no, not forged, melted into one course, all melted together, who can still eat that? Here is the menu, whatever you want you can have, but I can't give it to you, for I am the meal itself. I am the body of Christ, whoever eats of me, will certainly have what's most nouvelle on his plate, he can be sure of that. It will be burnt somewhat, but no one will have tasted it before. The community comes forward and receives the body of the Lord, that is, whatever is left of the community, it isn't much, but so much for the exclusivity of the human meal as well as of the Son of Man meal, a supper, a *Nacht-Mahl*, a night meal. No doubt. An honest-to-God night-meal. A man's night-mate. *You* will swear oaths and break them, that you will eat here every week, that's how good it is. You will pay for it. *You* will pay for everything. The money will be the only winner in the end. The hero will be dead, the money will win. Still, the hero enters the competition of the foods of gods, he wouldn't have to, he could declare himself the winner, but he goes for it, not bad. Nevertheless, he will have to accomplish something. The children of the night forged the treasure, forged the ore, melted the cans and made new ones out of them, no, these were the children of the day, the children of the light, they make bags out

143

of plastic bottles, out of paper – which they have to glue together with some other crap or the whole thing would fall through – they make warmth which actually stays inside the house, they seal houses, they make practical lamps out of trash, they basically turn everything into trash, rubbish, if you will, but out of rubbish they make something beautiful again, something new, they know how to do that, they are good at that. They separate, they separate, they would even separate the Holy Trinity and make a single one out of it, if they could, the top would be made from a different substance than the body, which in turn will secrete another substance which you drink and you will also be all new again, the beverage for the last boundless, free feeding of humans. No longer will we have to eat bread and fish, we will be permitted to eat human flesh and all of it will be made out of the Holy Trinity, that's how it's done if you've got no can to trans-form. Such is the German hero. He never thinks of himself, he always thinks about how he can separate and connect again, how he can reconnect limbs he had sev-ered himself or weld abherents into something new, much more durable. This is how Germans make from something durable something more durable. And this is how they themselves could endure for so long, sticking themselves on to each other, not sticking it to each other, clinging to each other, and, clawed into each other, shouting and howling, they go up the creek, maybe even the entire Rhine, because they must pay for other coun-tries to boot, while they treat their own stuff so carefully, how carefully they separate their *Dreck*, but still they must pay, what did I want to say, okay, so they shout so loudly, they always shout loudly, the Germans, you hear them practically everywhere, they rage, they claw into each other, they clump together into one single piece of

144

hero and then they enter the dark empire of death, where everyone has to go anyway, only the Germans create such a brouhaha before, though they just have to pay, all they have to do is pay, not as before when they had to make more out of themselves, they have to pay only for others, but they make such a show of it, no, not this one, another one, be glad! Others might also try, they will try, now I don't know what any more, well, whatever, the others will try, but the Germans will know how, that is, only the hero will know how, but for the Germans the hero still is a hero. The German is the hero, like a can, he melted into a hero. But that's already one too many. Would they have divided themselves up, it might have been better. Even a god divided himself into three parts, but there were so many who would have also wanted a piece, the three parts were not enough. The German gets dealt out to the world and unfortunately there will always be too few of him, who always must pay a lot. For every German is a hero, that's what he thinks, and when they have to pay for others, those heroes, they think so all the more. They made such beautiful things out of trash, heroes, yes, all of them, definitely, they are heroes. Others just throw their stuff out, the hero makes something out of it and then he burns everything, except the cats. They are spared. There will only be *The German*, and his pet will be safe. Like commodities, we gods will traffic only among ourselves and our closest relatives, Papa. With hammer and sickle, with Donner and Froh, with this, what's his name, Loge, this German Prometheus who brings fire, not takes it, even to the gods, that's different for a change, Papa. What is due to us is our value, which we, however, know exactly beforehand. Because everyone wants it. That's what makes it so valuable. In order to keep mine, I quickly have to get the fire before the Germans have to pay, so that no one will come along who is not authorized, who does not have the authority to look for the cracks through which he could come, through loopholes in the law, what do I know. They didn't know either whom they sought when the maiden arrived and spoke the words of Jesus: I am whom you seek etcetera. That we have been approved for traffic just proves that we are practical, competent people. Something can be made out of them and they can make gold out of garbage. And then we have to pay again. It's always only us who get to pay! No one in his right mind would permit folks like us. But we are needed so that we can pay. We have the strict order to separate the trash, because only we can make something out of *Dreck* that is in demand. They all want our money, they all want our gold. But no one wants to work. Only we do the work. In this sentence – unfortunately it turned into two – I described the world and can finally stop. Glad that you welcome it! What I will still say are subordinate clauses, but not unimportant, you might find them stimulating rather than aggravating as usual and verily I say to you: we would rather separate from our kin than not separate the trash in our bins. We wouldn't get a thriving licence if we wouldn't do it. The energy requirement for the production of the body of a can out of two cans is high, the content risky, but it's worth it, the Consumer Product Safety Commision would lock us up, if the production of this can from iron and aluminium would not pay off for humanity, the iron settles in the body of the can, the aluminium is on top, yes, they would lock us up, if it would not pay off. First it must pay off, then we'll do it. He would scrap us, the god, the president, the CPSC, whoever, we would all have energy requirements to make more of ourselves. And those we spare ourselves.

If we had energy, we could spare us much more, we would not have to murder those two cans, we could rein-cannate them, we could make new Valkyries out of the energy , this task could also be taken on by pure energy, mind you, my sisters are not yet retired, they still work full time, not even part time, they fetch heroes, they clean up the tin mens, sorry, can't help it, the cans, they war, they weave, they work wonders, whatever, the he-roes are taken away on the horses to be recycled and readied for new fights like foxterriers, they also want to fight all the time, what did I want to say, look at this pro-spectus, Father. You don't have to deploy your daughters to the battlefields any more! Isn't that nice?! The cans don't have to be scrapped, their bodies don't stress the slopes any more, the people can die, no problem, they can be totally replaced now, we can try it on the Valkyries, one can buy the Valkyries, one can even buy something better than the Valkyries!, such as BEAR, the Battlefield-Extraction–Assist-Robot! He fetches the dead. He has a strong hydraulic system that picks up the dead, yes, the wounded too, even the ones where it's ap-parently not worth it any more, those whom my sisters would leave there, because no heroes could be made out of those, no one would do that, any can would outclass them, especially if you consider what can be made out of it, at least two cans, no, this bear robot picks up the dead, he picks up the heroes, he picks up those who aren't quite dead yet, he picks up all of them, without looking at the person, although he can see and he is quite a sight, he is very well constructed, well developed, the BEAR, he can also carry other heavy objects, but he doesn't have to, people can do that, it's not worth it with objects, but he can collect the dead in peace and quiet, the wound-ed too, no matter how maimed they are, he safely gets them all. Though in the military they say that he could also lift other, heavier stuff, objects, but it is more important to recover the dead and not die oneself doing it. Ask my sisters, Father, they have experience in this. You can also ask me. The Bear does the work for us, we become superfluous and the second can, which also contained fluid, does the throwing away of the first one for us and the new can which emerged from the old one is doing it, while the Bear advances from among us and recovers the dead, great!, cool aids both, especially when in the can and the can in the fridge!, and in that time we can do something more meaningful, Father. We can, as already said, separate the trash, we can separate from our loved ones, our love can separate from us and meanwhile the robot picks up the dead, he does the work we did before and long, long before, he replaces us with pinpoint precision, that's a fact, Father. You didn't have to conceive us, because this construction replaces us completely, in every field, over long distances and rough terrain such as stairs. The Bear even carries dead heroes up and down the stairs, which our horses would have never managed! That is neat, Father, I know no other word for it, but here is this word and it says: I am that which you seek. No, thanks. I don't need sentences either, because I don't know the one, the crucial sentence. Words I don't need either, even though I have none, I don't need them any more. A robot will also replace me and my little rant which I sing, not as the little woodbird, but as one who is cuckoo, that thing will also replace ranting little me in a much simpler way than us cadaver-carrying sisters. He'll be able to do that, the Bear. He is constantly in development and even now, as I am talking, he gets further developed, tomorrow he will already be better than today, absolutely. At first, humans were still needed to operate on the wounds, no, hold it, operators for the technology, for the Bear, right, but in the meantime he can do what we Valkyries do, all by himself, and more, much more, he can't just carry humans, he can carry much heavier things, but actually he was made for the dead, like most inventions which are to help humans and this one helps us. His hands are strong but also small and sensitive, precise enough to keep several balls up in the air, uhm, that is, to keep his balls at all, without dropping them. Anyway, isn't it neat, Papa! Many a hero of ours had no head on top, because we couldn't get a proper hold of him, because we almost treated him like a can, even though we were not authorized, we only were in charge of their transport, but that wouldn't happen to the Bear. And he has this cute teddybear face, can you see it before your one, albeit intellectual eye, he's got this cute bear face, so that he can give solace, and provide security to and rekindle confidence in those he rescued and recovered. We can't do that, Father, we must tell them that we only rescued them so that they can go on fighting for you. Yes, those rescued by the Bear's hand must do so too, but that cute face of their saviour, some Bear, he! will fool them. No, we won't get into such deceptions and misconceptions. A machine will replace us, getting better every day, Father. And listen, Papa, how it talks through us, how the Id talks, how our commodified soul, about which our hero, the do-it-yourself hero won't give a damn (he don't need no machine), how whoever will talk: wealth is a quality of humans, value is the quality of goods. A person is rich. The Pink Panther, the sparkling gem, later transformed into a plushy or just a projection on the screen, reproduced and given to the world as a substitute for the stone for which or with which they slay, shoot, knife and then blow up each

149

other and then get saved by a Bear robot, no, they aren't worth it, those won't be saved, even though they are heroes, but otherwise everyone else will be. Pink Paulchen – well, why not a panther, bear is good, panther is good too, if also more dangerous, every creature, let's put it this way, is valuable. But things are more valuable. Objects are more valuable. The thing is valuable. Everything that's a thing is valuable. Capeesh? Even if a person has to make it. The thing is valuable. One is more valuable than all the others. Maybe. Only people are the same or at least want to be. Though it's all the same to them if they aren't. They never manage anyway to become as different as objects. So then, different but exactly like it: the use value of an object emerges from the relationship of the object to the person, it's simply there, worth its weight, without anyone able to challenge him for it, to whom it might be more valuable, whereas its exchange value emerges only in said exchange, that is in the process of being called on stage and thus more valuable than sitting in the dressing room in his underpants or whatever, of galloping towards the virgin and saving her, of dragon killing, giant killing, boar killing or whatever they want to kill, value emerges only there, the actual value, for which they bash in each other's heads, the value, for which we all will die though not before we have paid for all the others, Papa, and then we'll all be saved by a robot in bear form. That's how it will end. I don't agree at all with your actions, Father, wanting someone else for me, who is to do this until he himself is done in, take himself to the market, which is not even possible, become my guardian, which is not even possible even though his will dwells inside him like the hunter in his raised blind, on his high horse, in a bind. A machine could do all this, it could probably even oil its own joints. So, where does that leave common sense? It looks in from above and covers its eyes. The high ground, from where one looks down and which Frau Waltraud, who brought us good tidings and who is also a great new customer – I bet you already forgot her, but I won't permit it!, – will absolutely do without it now in our show, as she jumps into a pool filled with water, a voluntary task, which is actually the main task, so that her body under her clothing can be seen even more clearly or for some other reason which is not transparent to me – unlike the clothing of this woman when it got wet – but which the hero knows or he would not have pulled this on her. The hero wants to see what he already sees anyway. But what he sees must make sacrifices, for him. Jesus sees everything anyway, but we have to work hard to make him see what he sees anyway and would always see. And on others, Jesus, or rather, the deputy of Jesus, no, not the Pope, he's much too old for that anyway, just as some victims of Pink Paulchen Panther were too old, it is rather unlikely that they would still procreate, so we rather kill those who could procreate, still procreate new Others, completely different new Others who are exactly as different, as their name already tells us, they must be shut off, switched off, we would have had many opportunities to kill, but all the victims were too old, so then Jesus Christ, the hero, now I don't know any more who, some other hero, would pull something different. But he would never pull down the curtain on himself. He wants to be adored after all. He wants to pull it off, whatever it may be. He will succed in having someone castrate or mutilate himself some other way in front of the camera. But drawing the curtain on himself he never would. He will perform again and again, whatever happens, it doesn't happen to him, after all, but of course he would do it to others. And that will be totally normal. Everything will be normal. One man will totally meet the dreams of Frau Waltraud, but therefore also of all the other women and become her hero. The end of the world will come, the hero is already looking forward to it, therefore it must come. And I will finally also get my hero. He won't be interested at all in the fire in the trailer, he will simply step over it. Someone will castrate himself in front of the camera, I see it coming. He will do it himself, he won't need a murderer, an assistant or artificial grip arms. So then he can even imagine the loss of his member, but I can't imagine the loss of nothing, the Nothing I have and am. And the Nothing would happen exactly as I say, Father, the Nothing, if he were not permitted on stage, if he were not permitted anything, if he were not permitted to make himself stand out, to show off, if the self-castigator, I mean castrator, the self-collector of his own member, so that he can't procreate any more, else he would be murdered, easy does it now, (he takes his own member, so that he can't procreate and get killed, obviously), so then if this self-mutilator of his own member would not be allowed onto the stage, even though he worked so hard, jumping up the few stairs to the stage all by himself, if he is not permitted to do that then I don't know what will happen, the humiliation thereby created would not be bearable for anyone. This man must not take himself apart, even though he would do it himself, even though he would do something un-imaginable only I could imagine. Anything that protrudes somehow, of course even the prostrate gland, must go, he gets rid of it and then he is not permitted to mount the stage and ride off with it, because it would be gifted to him for his brave defiance, for what else could it be used after that? He would be allowed to take it home with him, the stage, because the feat he accomplished could never be surpassed. I, however, have nothing left to lose, Father. The boys do something one does not approve. They are told and right away they do it. Now all the more so. I am not even told so. I have no part, I mean, I don't have that kind of part and I must not have part of it and I get robbed, and I don't even know of what. Only your leaving, Father, that's all I know. And that I should forget you, the ultimate castration, Father, forgetting you, getting pulled into the Nothing that is oneself. I am nothing, I am a nothing. I know it. You gave me the horse, but I have to share it with my sisters. What, they already have their own? Saving already for the hot Bear aggregate? That was really nice of you, Papa. They are still afraid of you, would never go against you. Of course you would give each a horse. We already have a whole riding stable filled with them, each one wanted her own, save the stallion, no, save the pawn you received from a member of our audience!, that's all what us girls must take care of. But in the future, all of this would just be sports. The horse isn't all that'll wait for me, behind the fire. Someone else is waiting there or he comes right away. No wonder every girl wants to learn how to ride right away, before she can even walk properly. I want more, I want sport! I want still more, but am becoming less and less. This less of me the hero will replace, this is what you promised me, Papa! You promised me that he will come, the hero, whatever I have to imagine this to mean. Okay. I get the fire, only one will get through there. After all, that's why it's there, the fire. It even was my idea, and my ideas aren't bad, Father. But not even I would have thought up something like this robot, attaboy!, storming up the stage like that pink cat, but he does not kill, he rescues. He rescues one hero at a time. One made it. He will be hunted for years, the Germans love to do that, it's their favourite hobby, but he will get through it, as the only one. He will have been the elect even before he could get erect. Then he will be uninteresting. He will be one of many. The poor dwarf too, we don't even talk about him any more, of course a dwarf can be more easily replaced than a hero or a hero's female stretcher bearer, a hero's corpse bearer, the dwarf will have expired, there he was, learning how to forge for such a long time and then he gets booted out, because only the hero forges the sword. Father: you originated the heroes, you can do with them whatever you want, onstage or off, in the anonymity of the many. Begotten by the brain of the Earth you can do whatever you want, you can even make the hero, he too originates from you. You can do it all. Yes, your breath originates from you too, your sperm: from you too, your spirit, your courage: from you too. Everything from you. You exhale so much, that the hero is not able to inhale it all. You've got only one eye, Father, but it shines, even without lights and camera. The other eye in the sky. Who cares. The dwarfs are ruined, the giants tamed by eternal envy, they are called humans now, if they are still alive. I understand all of this, Papa, and yet: I get extracted from myself like seeds albeit not for me, I get expropriated, the *Schatz* won't have any positive effect on me either. I will have seen the hero like a light and then become a light myself, albeit a little one. On logs of my own failure shall I kneel. That'll be rather bad for me. Effect: negative. On others even more so, but on me especially strong. My *Schatz* will have a negative effect. A noble gaze at women is nothing yet to give it any thought, but when they are used, they often get into an awkward situation. They get into a credit crunch, a sudden shortage

154

of themselves, and yet they want to be generous. Mother, what says she? Mother Earth, what does she have to say to this? Surely, she must have her say! I'd think she wouldn't mind one less of us trampling on top of her, now that the robots are already coming to stress her, the next generation whose special property it is that there will always will be several generations of them, just following each other in shorter intervals than a mother could ever accomplish, while humans always get into extended rows. Mother Earth, what does she say? Anyone can throw a few chunks of her after him, but lifting the whole earth he can't, much too heavy, even the Bear can't do it. One escapes her, even though she is her child. She won't suffer from empty nest syndrome, Erda will never suffer, even though she often claims she does, she'll never suffer, she doesn't suffer us foolish children, but she does not suffer; she's still got three stay-at home-daughters with their rope, with their golden rope, gold everywhere, matter of fact, gold is all I see everywhere, tell me, Papa, have I gone crazy throwing away so much gold? Everywhere gold and it belongs to no one and yet, everyone claims it for himself. Strange material. Not made by Mama Earth. Or was it? Taken out of Mama Earth, born from her womb, like her children? Children of the Earth? Gold that changed its form, now forged into a ring, funny, so let's calculate how much has been consumed during its processing! It can be calculated with perfect precision. Let dwarfs stand in for us at the instruments of labour laid out for us. Someone had to have done it, someone must have produced it, the surplus value, someone must have procured the higher value. Now we do the counting and calculating, yes, you can count on us, but not always. But we calculate that a certain mass of gold flowed into the product of labour (for our Pink Panther: a real diamander), okay, let's say, the result of two hundred days of labour, something like that, I have no idea, how long this kind of thing takes, at any rate, it follows that those, let's say, two hundred days of labour have been objectified in the ring, for the gold has changed its form, right, because nobody could have carried off those tonnes of gold, anyone can wear the ring, although he'd better throw it out, he does take a risk, because the ring might not fit, might be too big, too heavy, provoke perplexity and disbelief among his friends, but he wears it. Anyone can carry on with a ring, the bigger the better. And if not, we also carry the sword, the horse and the hood, of which I don't quite know what it can do, even though it was shown to me, that is, nothing was shown to me; it doesn't show, the hood, actually, no one sees anything, but you can't tell from a can either what can become of it and what's more: no one's supposed to see you in that hood. No, then it can't be seen either. With some hoods it certainly wouldn't be a drawback. And with me it would have been better anyway, I should have taken the other one, it looked better on me. The sword: even the sword escapes the scaffold, I mean the scabbard, even the sword has its protection, it is carried inside it. It doesn't thrash around. Rather it is used for thrashing around. Many herogues have to battle with it. Only I? Only I have to and get nothing? I hear nothing and am nothing? More protection for the sword than for me? Then the fire, okay, I made it work for me, but I did not invent it, that was Loge, he brings it to the gods. Prometheus went the other way around, the result is always the same: a disaster, but mind you, the guarding of the fire, even in my sleep has become my job in the meantime anyway. Always been there, it feels like to me. Fire: nothing fundamentally new to me. It's all organic products I am dealing with. Others I reject. Bio. Pure bio. Very important. Keeps one healthy behind the fire that scorches the earth, slowly but surely. But it can all go quite quickly suddenly.

W: Away from me, yes! It is true what they always say: only fire is not obedient. The daughter obeys, the fire doesn't. The loss of fire can be imagined, but to constrain it, to tame it, that's a lot of work in the Swedish wood stove. The father torn out of the daughter, now only a silhouette, put up against the wall, a photo, once child of the light, now torn out, no longer thrilled by property is he, erased in himself the daughter he raised, immeasurable power was his, not any more, deprived of his daughter, it hurts me as much, but it doesn't show. The wanderers, I, also a wanderer, walk past the riches of others who always feel threatened by lack, the deprivation that is, they caused the others. The great riches of the ones, also of the gods, I am no longer one of them, so then the great riches of the ones, of some, the few, the always fewer, are always accompanied, unlike the wanderer, by the absolute deprivation of the essential necessities of life for many others. It says so right here. And there I stand, child. Part with me you must, deprived you shall be, like the many, choosing your side I am not free to do. That's how it is, look at it the other way, with my eyes, not always these accusations! Let me tell you, parting with you is something else, it is to be without something, but allowed to keep everything, just not the one. That's not pleasant for a god. Having everything, free to give everything, except for just one thing, not free to keep the one, the daughter, that's pretty tough. It doesn't just rankle god. But it must be, because the

157

adult leaks, the adult leaks out, because he can't tame his desires, on the contrary, what he desires is only taken away from him, the athlete goes beyond himself, but the adult ends with the child. He ends himself through the child. He practically leaks out. The child expropriates him around itself as the capitalist expropriates the labourer. He leaves him just about enough so that he can live, as the father leaves the child only enough so that it lets him live better. Alimony gets paid, working hours are fulfilled, the little plant gets watered, but its never enough to extinguish the fire. Folks simply want to burn all the time, they are always on fire for something, dying for something, whatever, they always want to have the ultimate fire, to get the ultimate, or they wouldn't be them, yes, and the child is also part of it, the child is the utmost there is, and thus so many want to have one, but I give my child to the fire, which was her own idea, she complains. She always complains. Why do you do that? What's hurting you now? Just keep writing, then nothing hurts. Nag nag nag! Stop it already! A hero will show up for sure. If no hero would come, I could not get away from you, I'd have to come up with something for the hero to fall, because the hero, especially if he's dead, also elevates me. Increases my army. Elevates me and falls for you. I give him to you, but you must wait. Sadly, you will have to wait until he is dead, nothing to be done about that. Please check the departure screen in the departure terminal. Please wait for the announcements on the station platform! In the meantime, you can write your heart out, if the train to the top is late. You always do that anyway. And the sword you want to keep? Of all things I should let you have it? It could be three times as big and five times as unbreakable, you'd still not become a man because of it. You get very close to the ideal, fair enough, I have to admit it. You will be engaged to the hero, engaged and enamoured, if disarmed, married I don't know, I don't see it yet, don't know if it'll be this one, who is a doer of deeds, he may have to leave sooner, before he can marry you, here we call him hero, elsewhere God. Because of his inevitable death, the power will drop back into its bed, its fluid bed. The treasure will return to those to whom it always belonged, who always had it, they will get the treasure again. I made everything, you and the ideal and that which you leave behind, I made it all, as Father, but I didn't make the money, I always had to get along with the money, as it comes from the outside, I mean, I had to enter into contracts on its behalf and in the end everything was as in the beginning. Those who had it have it again. Everything that has been, that will be, no one tells me any more, but I know what will happen, I know that all methods of raising the social productive power of labour – by the way, and that's really just a sidenote – the most terrific productive power there is, but it does not belong to those who have it, they lend it, they give it away if necessary, while they could do so much with it!, where was I, that all methods of raising the productive power of labour are thus put into effect at the cost of the individual labourer, of the respective person, that all means for the development of production transform themselves into means of domination over, and exploitation of the producer. Everything turns out badly, fortunately for the unfortunate producer, for he doesn't need a fortune, others worry about that and let that be his good fortune. This is one of those tipping processes, I know, child, you are waiting for your hero, who will also tip over soon. Whatever humans do affects them to their disadvantage and less to their advantage; and the people, the workers are mutilated into fragments of humans. I never did that, I, warrior, who, though, never gets the wares, not made for it. It was me, after all, who had to shell out for my new house, but I prevented nothing. I as a god did not prevent it. I made, but I did not prevent. Actually, I never made anything that hadn't been there already. And those who had it all still have it. I simply have had it. I don't want to be too tough on myself: the I, yes, this I, I did make somehow, but only for me, what good did it do me?, none, I made the Id, what good did it do me?, none, not even others did it any good, but maybe it is you, the Id, child, but also just for me. Because we also make children only for ourselves, at least we can keep those, sooner or later they too will be appendages of a machine, they'll even beg to become become appendages of a machine, which, however, will no longer exist. There will be people, but too few machines for everyone. There will be ever more people than machines. And then there will be machines, but they will serve the people, they will fetch the dead from the battlefields, nobody will have to get in harm's way for the sake of a dead or wounded and soon the machines themselves will fight, they will fight each other, then no one will have to die any more either, oh God, what will we do then with all those people?!, no opportunity any more to waste them, recycle them, make hummus out of them for bread for the world, but not for the people; I, the God, will spare myself the dying, yes, that'll work, I am sure, me staying, and the dying of others will end as well and you too, child, have already been rationalized away. You'll be jobless then, the unpowered power for something. As far as I am concerned you can also be something else, even everything else, anything else, for all I care, that's got a name but doesn't mean it. You can be anything, but you are not a man and never will be. You can be anything, but not a man, at least not this one, but I think, not anyone else either. You are always the one who buries heroes, but not the one who kills them. This highly esteemed part which you never name but desire, I am sure of that, which you want, even if you are niceness incarnate, that's not the way to get it anyway, and in any case, no one deprived you of it, because you never had it. Get used to it. The hero will trust that you simply know such things. When it comes to the vows, you will have to know. Okay, you are getting very close to it, having a highly esteemed part, here, for example, you have the sword, *a Notschwert*, emergency sword, I called it, for just that kind of situation, so take the sword, for you will sleep alone in a No-Man's land, let's call it *Notung* now, permit me: *Notung*, no, no one permits, let alone I, and you shouldn't either, don't permit it, permit nothing!, yes, take it, take good care of it, don't let anyone take it away from you! Hold it!, I just noticed, that's the wrong weapon you're clenching like a broomstick, the point is blunt, the writing is no good, that's not a sword, the quill a sword?, that's some joke! I forgot, who's got the sword now, probably the hero, one of them must have it, after all. What I put in your hand: I only said, it is a sword. But it isn't. Something must be put in your hand so that you don't play with or on yourself – that's what your stupid writing is all about ! – and forget the flames that surround your sleep, there is no cure for it, this sleep comes from a herb, a poison or it comes because I put my hands on your eyes, that was enough. It won't be enough for the hero, he'll want you to adore him starry-eyed, for this my eye in the sky might be useful to you, so take it then, the Father's eye. Maybe it'll help. Women always have to fall asleep even before something is about to happen, in the bushes, behind hedges, behind fires, behind water, in the woods, in the pastures next to the animals, in the wombs of animals, well that at least they would have to notice!, but no, they always sleep, the sleeping, not the slaphappy sex. In their free time they sleep. When they are free, they also sleep. They always sleep, even when they bend over backwards, they sleep, piling up the heavy logs is someone else's job, they are too weak for that, of course. Then they poke around in the embers or they peek through a shining window that opened up for them, into the world. You will not hear children whining when they break or spill something. Without fruit you shall remain for the hero without fear. Sleep. That's women's career. Sleeping. That's what I keep saying. So sleep. Play it as it lays, you won't win anyway. I've got to go. I turn my back on the back-talker who keeps claiming and complaining. That's easy enough. Over there, the claims. They all fit on one single ash stick, which then kicked the dust struck by a sword, not any old sword, THE sword!, they can't be that big then, those claims. Here I am, there I dwell to shoot them all down, I just turn my back, very easy. I don't mind at all. I am going. So. No problem for me, the caregivers act as if it were one, but it isn't. I can be everywhere at once, but they always look for me some other place. No problem, going, for the practised wanderer. Okay, with his one eye he might no longer be able to properly gauge distances, but move he can. The father leaves, that's nothing. Among all his activities, it is the easiest. No effort, really, please, it's no effort for me to walk away from you, child. It is like doing nothing. It is nothing. I am going. Around you fire, which I made. I had help, but it is burning because I wanted it that way. Anyone gets through, but only one knows it. A man,

162

peaceful like murder. Okay, now it keeps burning, all on its own. You don't have to do anything. You don't even have to extinguish anything. You don't even have to take food from the grill. The fire extinguisher does not follow the rule, according to which it was filled, doesn't matter, it is meant to burn, or it has been emptied in the meantime and put there again, the extinguisher, no idea, but in any case there's nothing in it now. Among the boys the nightly effusion, water under the boys, water, not grist on my mills in the active sinful hand. The boy works on himself, he plugs away, but the father just goes away. He is not interested in what the sons are doing, except when they bear arms doing it. The daughter sleeps. Nice family. But anyway, to each his own. Something like that practically melts in your mouth. The money's in the bank, the sum is entered in the shaft, also who gets how much. But I must not know what you wish for when you can't wet your lair, not even that, to extinguish the fire. With what? Which general rule do we impose on the fire-extinguisher, which doesn't function, even though its function is clearly defined when the sparks fly and jump. There can be no rule for the fire, for the fire is just a sign, a general notion which I am specifying now, though the fire-extinguisher is still empty. Nothing comes out of it. I found out through experience that it is empty. It is so light. Even with you, I say this before I try it out, nothing comes out of you as it does of the wetting boy. That's a misunderstanding. It isn't even a wetness! Still. With a boy, at least something comes of it! But with you: nothing. You can do what you want, child, nothing's coming. The fire I give you. Given. What you are going to do with it is up to you! But I am afraid for this you will need the hero. Your fire-extinguisher is down, no need to get it up and running, it doesn't function anyway and you wouldn't know what's up with it. You don't want another one and would not take any. That hero will cost you a lot. He will cost you everything you saved yourself up for. But the fire you can have for free, it is our own advertisement supplement to the rules we set up. The light is nothing but the ad for the gods. Your complaint supplement that your Papa does not lay with you, the fire, that is Papa's advertisement supplement one throws out without looking at it, a colourful piece of paper, a rag, a surplus, of no use for anything, all-said, a non-starter. By the time you start something with some-one who isn't me, by the time you catch on and catch someone who is not a disease, I mete out the punish-ment. The one who comes through, depending on the view, Jesus or a Mister Bakunin, depends on who knows whom, it's totally up to the viewer, no idea who they are, but this is the one to whom you give the ring. No, it makes no sense for you, I already explained it to you, to have the fire-extinguisher ready! When that man shows up, he gets the ring, period. He'll probably have it already. What you could give him, he's got already. Or he will have no use for it. Nevertheless, he will be proud of it in secret. Okay. So you give him the ring. Or not. Ridiculous. It doesn't matter. This time no beating be-cause of the spilled tea on the period furniture with the curved drawers filled with stuff no one needs, or it would not have been in style, the period piece with the bellied drawer something trickled into. This time no physical punishment all over again. I am going. Locking you up in sleep like the fluid in the nightstand, that flowed into it, oh no, and hot too!, that increases the punishment, ruining the veneer of this beautiful and expensive night-stand that got soaked, it once was expensive, I can't remember when and how expensive, but there it flows

164

in, the tea, the hot fluid, meant for wellness, turned into illness, pain, oh no, expensive piece of furniture full of tea, what were you thinking, when you knocked it over, when your hand missed it? That's the last place we need tea! You really could have been careful, here we value and honour our things, they once were expensive. You just have to reach anywhere and bingo, you find something that was expensive. Spilling tea in your sleep, that's no good. The boy, look, isn't he beautiful? The basically passive genital, that's meant to wake up – he never misses it, the boy, he always finds it, even in his sleep. But you, child, you don't even find the handle of the cup, the hand slips, there, now you have it and there it flows. But it doesn't come out of you. This fluid is not from you and yet it is now on the Caucasian walnut veneer. You reach for the handle of the cup and there it all pours into the precious little piece, it flows into the daughter but the boy has it flowing out of him. Simple as that. The boy at least comes up with something! For anything flowing, albeit in the wrong direction, only one thing is certain: always downhill, you get thrashed, nothing you can do about it. That piece of furniture was expensive. That calls for punches if it gets marred. Even though those stupid giants worked for free, that's at least how it was planned to be, at least by us, not by them, in the end everything was very expensive for us. We gave everything. It was expensive, what they made, and they made every single piece in the house. Each piece a gigantic job, yes, also this little chest, it is small but takes all the more work that wants to be paid for, maybe not wants to but has to. The fire here costs me nothing. In any case, you won't be defenceless when you will be awakened. This is the sword that isn't one, there is the horse no one can see, here I am no longer the one you

165

saw just now, soon the hero will come, who will get you or not. He will decide. He will recognize you. You will see him. Today I finally see a hero, you would say. But no one there to cart him off. Your sister? Which one? Or you won't see him, the hero, even though you have both your eyes and a piece of mind. You won't recognize him right away because you will have lost his photo. You better not have pasted it to the nightstand at home, that's all we need! You will recognize him or you won't. He will recognize that you are a woman, that'll be enough for him. A pretty simple hero, but a complicated one would certainly be more complicated than that small piece of furniture at home! That should do for him, you being a woman. A hero is he who recognizes whatever it may be, but also a hero is he, who does not recognize. He doesn't have to. He can't deal separately with everyone, I mean, he can't kill everybody, he can right a wrong, he can absolve from sin, he can redeem, but he can't do everything. A hero is everything, but he certainly can't do everything! A hero is still more. And you will be defenceless. You will have the sword, no, you will have what you take for a sword, maybe a ski-pole, a lipstick, eye shadow, eyebrow pencil, a steering wheel, no, not thinking, the difficulty with thinking is making it easy for oneself and still remaining precise, exact, get to the point; *'der Mensch denkt, aber Gott lenkt'* man thinks, but God steers, as we say or *Man proposes, God disposes*, as others put it, which does not work with my point – okay, so God does the steering, unfortunately in your case just a subcompact, which even you will be able to drive, yes, you will also have the horse, you will also have the fire, but you didn't make any of it. Everything you've got, will be given to you. It will be second hand, albeit a god's. You will be needed, and you will be used, someone will always use

166

you, that is your fate, needed and used. How awful! No, I am bowing out now! I don't want to be used by a *Frau* only because she wants to be needed! Okay, easy to say, one can say anything, but it will be impossible, because one can't penetrate the rules because there is no beyond. As for me, I only want to pick up myself. That is to say I only want myself. The hero can't possibly take on my guilt as well, any other but not mine. There is nothing he can do about that. He won't be able to stop me at the door to the spirit shop. Never shall opening hours enslave me, there will no longer be slaves, none at all, there will only be love, say Jesus and this Bakunin whose name was especially written down for me, even though they don't say it in the same words. All this will be brought on by the hero, but I can certainly do it also without him. No one will be able to enslave anyone, since they are also open on Saturdays until eight p.m. Since they will be open for anything.

B: Papa, don't go! Before you do, you still have to promise me a few things, I wrote it all down like everything, that's why I have to write all the time, and still I think of more and more I want: you can't just go like that. How can the loss of something that can't be seen strike so hard? How come? Mother's breast has already been denied to me, okay, I could get over that, I trampled on Mother Earth instead, but the loss of my strength I won't have the strength to bear. Yes, Papa, I know that it doesn't come from me, you gave it to me, like everything. I know. I am nothing and yet I once was everything, when I didn't yet know that I am nothing. I must part from everything, from it all! Everything wants to go. This purity in the fire demands some mighty sacrifices, Papa! Did that really have to be? You said, I have to get through this. But do I really? That I won't have any more germ cells, that I will be sterilized, that I will be totally sterile? That before that I must give away everything else just to get this, which I will owe you forever because I don't affect anything all on my own. Look, how they laugh at me! Because I affect nothing! What I can do is nothing, nothing, nothing compared to what others can do, who, though, must first be threatened with castration until they can do it, that's a horrible threat, oh yes, at least it can be very unpleasant, but with me they fall on deaf ears with this kind of thing. They, on the other hand, can do everything. You and the boys, you can do it all, the boys who are not dear to me, but should be dears. From the boy who was so dear to me...something...something from his hill so freshly green, yea, that's how it goes, a poem and also a *Lied*. Something is supposed to come from him, or he better come right away, the boy, any boy. No idea. I only live courtesy of others anyway, Papa. So why not? Why not exhaust oneself in masturbation, in burrowing in the Nothing? Why not be exhausted already before, by oneself, before the hero comes? There is nothing else to do behind the fire, Papa! No matter who's coming. No, not I, I am already here, a hero shall come, you promised me. One who sets everyone free, *frei*, without the *Arbeit*, the labour. This one creates no work, doesn't give the works and is no work. A fine piece of work: freer and *Freier*, a wooer on fire, who does not fry me, but frees me. Look, no one else could replace you, so give me this hero, give him to me, he will find me here! Tell him that! Promise me! Promise me the redeemer, Father! It doesn't cost you anything, he has already been promised so often, houses were built for him, opera houses!, yours is a dog house by comparison, and did he come? No. No one expects that he will really come. And he never really comes.

W: I have to move on, child. I have to move ahead as a spectre. As an undead. Can't stay any longer. Everyone conspired against this spectre. Ye wretched ones, one more time, wake up! Rise!, you can lie down again right after. We are a workers' party. Therefore a lot of hard work is going on here. Look, how I keep the fire going! It's very easy, with the tip of my spear, my Nordic-Walking-Pole, the smokestack is lit, the iron melts and if even iron melts, one can demand a lot of people as to what they should be able to do. And the workers tremble and the masters tremble and the bride trembles, the earth trembles, the Pink Panther trembles, he is the funniest trembler of all, ten times he has killed so far, but the desire to kill has not yet been satisfied, no, not in Paulchen! He is an earthquake, a pretty small-scale tremor, it happens only here, elsewhere they don't notice anything at all. What a blast! The ninth shot! No words, deeds! National Socialism all new, a little socialism, but all the more *national!* Emphasis added. Let's be concrete here. Concrete lies on this road. Deeds instead of words. People, carefully selected, and then suddenly it's others that get killed, that is, those who just happened to be there. *Alles für Deutschland.* The mobile phone rings. Cars pass by, a black BMW. I am just taking a shit, says the one hero. The other: So they aren't yet at your place. No, they don't dare, says the one hero. Why should they be afraid of you, thus number two. Well, because then two will bite the dust, again hero numero uno, who doesn't mean the second one. Here you have addled, or rather, added *Heldenworte*, hero words, here they are safekept, because they really didn't want to stay, the words, but that's a no-go, they won't get away from me!, here – it won't be often that *you* can read these words – here, then, Germania's *Heldenworte* are spoken and kept: no monkey business, hero! When they ring the bell, you better open, *Held*! And then you say: What do you want. Just as the hero maiden will say: I am whom you seek. So, and now the *Deutsche Gott*, the only one, albeit not the true one, now I am talking to my daughter and everybody else keep your mouth shut throughout!, so then: as long as no additional changes are requested by me, child, wilfullness will be the way to wait and work on the victims and the way to go will be with anything on wheels that still move, yes, even mountain bikes, we can wait and you will sleep that long. The hero won't learn to fear, because Germania did not learn about fear either, then why is she afraid of everything?, the poor country, why then is she so afraid of everything?, she is fearful all the time and yet she is so efficient, no need for her to be afraid, she could simply wake up, like you, child, soon, no, maybe somewhat later after all!, please wait, we will be there as soon as we can, and if not, then just let it bleed. And at some point Deutschland will shed it, the fear, which is all she knows, fear, which she leads behind her like a horse, but some day she will jump on it and flip the bird, and off she goes. And then, you will learn to shiver, to rise, at what price!, so high, you could hardly raise it any more, others could rise, but they don't do it. Deutschland, awake! How come you don't wake up? Because the gods are also sleeping? Because the favourite star got sick? Because this huge show which shines brighter than my eye in the sky has to wing it without him today? Because this or that guy can no longer be captain of the national team? So we take another one! In any case, there will be an awakening, no matter who with whom. No matter who will take part. All of them are right somehow, but it doesn't do them any good, as long as I have the right. As soon as the ring will have been rightfully returned, they will praise me, the Father, that won't cost them anything any more, on the contrary, they will have cashed in on the latest prohibited substance, the tickets to the *Dämmerung*, the twilight on the mountain, which lets a fortress stand on it, whatever. Tomorrow it will be another substance they will take. They will sing and sing that I am the mighty All-Father and Germany the *Über Alles*, all this won't cost them an arm and a leg any more. Why, they already have the ring. It will always be there and always unchangeable, because the girls can't reforge it. It stays as it is. Everything stays as it is. That's called a revolution here. Those who had it will get it again. Always the same. Nothing will cost any more. But if it won't cost the daughters, it won't cost anyone anything and no one will listen to me, the All-Father, no, not Father *über alles* in the universe, that would be too big for me, but if it is about as big as Germany, it remains surveyable: our Father, our Father in heaven, no, Father of all, let's put it that way. As long as there are no fundamental changes, there will be murdering and murdering and murdering. No matter who goes for it or what they have to go through because of it. Dragons, giants, humans. Everyone who comes to my mind must come to an end. They all get killed. Until no one is left who does the work. An unpleasant situation. Who'll clean our dirt now? I am still here, but I was not hired for cleaning. Those who clean are far below me, vanished in the fog just like the fortress. A spectre doesn't die and has nothing to fear. I, myself, have nothing to fear. The little bomb that could, on tour in Germany. A Hit! Wow! What an act! Little Pink Panther's latest pranks, this time in moving and quite moving pictures. Power radiates from deeds not words, I am the spectre that's haunting you, I am Jesus, no, the hero is Jesus, or Anarcho-Bakunin, depends on what you read, depends how nice you want to be; I am God Father, but we are anyway, nice, yes, also the Ghost, but we don't need him, we are at one and one. I enter the words in you, child, that you, too, can be Jesus, if you want to be. When the hero gets through the fire, that is, when he will have gone through the fire for you, you simply say to him what Jesus said back then: I am whom you seek. You don't have to say, let the others go! Not necessary at all. No others will be there. Not at that time. Only a few cops, that's all. Others will come, more of them, well, they first have to be told what happened. They wouldn't see it, not even if it would happen right in front of their eyes. At that time, however, the colleagues of the Nothing, its best friends, they'd want nothing more than to be the Nothing themselves, will already blaze away brightly, no, they will have been shot by themselves and set on fire, which they diligently spread themselves all over the place before. The global conflagration. The school of the global conflagration. That's where they wanted to be put. That's how they imagined it. But I don't want others beside myself to still be there. A god gets beside himself, when he sees others beside himself, they seize something much too big for their size. They even manipulate the measuring tape to seem bigger! That doesn't work. I always felt awkward having people right beside me, strangers, even though I created all of them as well. Only you, the sleeping Germany, the holy Germany, the Germany that won't then be locked any longer into labour and production branches and hasn't been for a long time already, on the contrary, its branches keep growing gracefully, its markets open wide and far, it constantly eyes others, but it is still locked up in itself, just elsewhere, nobody notices it, nobody takes note of it, nobody takes notes about it which might prove useful later, but everyone would notice if it wouldn't be there any more and I don't know either at the moment where it went now. But this time it certainly isn't gone for good, kaput, ailing. I would know that. On the contrary, it gets celebrated. In any case, it is no longer where it produces its fridges and washing machines and then puts them elsewhere, at this time I don't see them there any more, it is most certainly locked in its TV programme, yes, there it is , no doubt, no, not dubious, I can see that, since no one else wanted to see this programme, not even as a present; it is locked in its handy devices, their *Handy* as they call it, maybe that is why it is so bad, because it never gets out, never opens the door, never at least once gets out of its devices which, however, were made elsewhere. It is locked up in Europe, Germany in Europe, except that Europe itself is locked at this time, doesn't matter, it is locked in its games which it plays with itself, at which it stares, who's winning?, it no longer knows what that is, it no longer knows what labour is, but to whom it belongs it certainly knows, and if it knows nothing any more, that it knows. And when no one knows his way in or out and confuses entrance and exit, then, yes then it will wake up, this Germany which I, however, would no longer want to get to know, the old one was enough for me. Maybe Europe, but I don't know. I don't yet see it at this time. I'm old and have one eye only and no spatial vision, I said it a few times. Germany, however, will always be wide awake, even before it wakes up. When it will know nothing about itself any more and when millions will shout in its ears, it will wake up, then it will fork out the millions. And those teaching it the wound of knowing: someone's gotta do it. Then it knows what's up and whom it brought down. Deutschland: I am whom you seek, that is what you will say, what my hero maiden will say, in the words of the Lord Jesus which he spoke in front of the shelf with the adulterated olive oil. And your fight will start with your new existence, child, let's say, like the workers' fight against conditions of production, it doesn't matter who is fighting, pardon me, he doesn't exist, the worker and the conditions are ludicrous, often I don't read through my own regulations very carefully, because I've known for a long time what's what; I look at everything through the lens of calculation and I am the calculator operating as laid down in strict rules, the main thing is that they lie there and sleep tightly, like you, child, but my terms, in case *you* ask for it, no, *you* don't, I am not whom *you* don't even seek, that is my daughter, so then, I know and I determine for the others: the worker does not exist any more and there are no longer conditions of production. But Germany still exists and they are very good at it there. Germany, awake! Oh dear, I see, I slipped one line too high or one paragraph too low, I don't find it any more, and furthermore: who's supposed to read it all, this stuff my daughter concocts, or rather copies here, who knows from whom? It's all been worked out long ago who will control whom. No need for me to read it all! You, dear customer of home appliances have also tuned out long ago. And *tschüs*! It doesn't matter. Eternal sleep is all there is. Like yours, child. Germany sleeps. But whatever it does, whatever it makes when it awakes, it will make out very well for sure. Germany, awake! Didn't you hear me before, when I first requested it? I think it will also keep watch quite well. It won't go wacko again when it wakes. No? No. Nothing. Please not that!

174

Sleeping forever or doing something very well, that's the trick I thought up for you all. An example, I just don't know for what, it might be a case for Inspector Bakunin, because Jesus could have never thought up something like this: the worker's fight against his master begins with his existence. Whose? Both? Probably. There can't be the one without the other, but whether they came about at the same time, well, I don't know that, I just pooped at that time. Or was I online? No idea. Your fight for your existence, daughter, starts with your sleep. You had a certain life before, that is turned off now. All of you, no matter who comes along and where he wants to go, will not get anywhere, not even awake and not either once the watchmen will let you out of your brain cells. And the fight will not end with the fight against the owners of the means of productions, but also against foreign, competing commodities. At this time, the fight is on against everything and everywhere. It is a fight any which way. A spectre haunts the world, and that's no longer a god, even if it is me, it is no one's god and I don't want to be a god now either. Now I am a has-been once and for all, and a spectre is both: the end and forever. There is no end to the spectre, because it cannot be checked out, it is seen too rarely. It passed on its ID long ago. So then I am the spectre, the haunting ghost. I am not a god any more. And I am the one to know it best. But putting you to sleep I can just about still manage. The workers smash the machines, they set the factories on fire, but what emerges here glowingly, maybe because so many fires were hurled? These words emerge: Made in Germany! They seek to regain the medieval worker's extinct position, if much too late and certainly not middling; that makes him into a mass splintered all over the world, a mass that would actually belong to

Germany, where the masses are valued on principle, especially when they keep running in the same direction, but they are splintered like my ash spear, like its shaft. Splintered. Fragmented. Expelled. Expelled by export, because no one buys that foreign junk any more. Only made in Germany gets bought. This car, this hair dryer, this food processing *Küchenliesl*. That's not the world, and it no longer costs an arm and a leg, though the most life-like artificial limbs are also made in Germany. But a bit more does have to be invested. There they stand and stream into the shopping centres and supermarkets, basically everywhere, only the markets of the world are closed to them. No, they are not. On the contrary, now you can get in anywhere. But every market is closed if you don't come as a consumer. You go to the outlet to get a new outfit, but you are also let out anytime. We don't use force, we are the force. If someone wants to buy something the market is open immediately, but only a small one, there is an outlet built for him in the fields, on top of Mother Erda, our earth, she can endure anything, what else could she do. The market is shut. Unfortunately, the market is closed now. Because of overfulfilment of our charges and bargains, our urges and splurges, the market must be shut out temporarily. I still don't understand what I am saying. But I must say it. Entire countries have to sell themselves, but nobody wants them. Everyone will want to have Germany, but Deutschland will want to have and hold on to itself. It will hold up and out all on its own. But it won't just hand out and over or it would not have become the export-world-champion. It is a hit, well, now, that beats everything, yes, the very top must simply be permitted! It will hold on to and at the same time export itself. There will be contradictions in our transactions and transfigurations, our figures, all the time, you can see that, but they all take place in Germany, that too stays between and with us and nothing is possible in place of Germany, there is no other place. Doesn't work. It cannot be replaced. Well, yes, the furnaces on the Ruhr don't roar any more, they are elsewhere now and fired up by others. Instead, this *Drogenmarkt*, this drugmarket, I mean, drugstore, has just announced its opening, don't ask me why. Every day the opening of at least two new markets. This one for example is at the service of all people as of its opening. They are in demand, these products, they received the excellence award from the Product Test Foundation, those are excellent products, always the same, cross my heart, nevertheless, I see fear in the owners: will people actually come to them or go right next door to exactly the same market, except something else is written above the portal. But nowadays it isn't so easy to catch people any more, they come through totally different portals, which can't even be seen. They are coming, here they come, but they are nothing. By shopping they become nothing. They remain nothing. In the width of the vast, they are nothing. That's because of their sheer numbers, the masses of them, there simply are too many, but no worry, they will get through some portal. They just have to split up. They don't have to split, they have to split up. Their stream must part or they crush each other. But only one is to rule. *Divide et impera*. Only one calls the shots. I. God. The end. All these portals lead to the end, patience, I'll get there too. I and the end, which I want and will bring about. Until only one will remain in the end, the end point of accumulation, as the workers' situation worsens to the extent capital is accumulated. The customers' situation improves, because there are so many products, the networks' situation improves, because nothing goes in the other direction, always only in and heavenly, no, heavily laden, weighed down, out again, the portal opens in one direction only, and everyone, everyone may get in, there is too little space in the world, but in space there still is plenty left. Hold it! Nonsense! If no one came out again, where would they all be then? I have to think about that some more. There is no time for it now, I have to write, after all. Nothing gets worse because of the new. Only the workers' situation gets worse, well now, I wouldn't put it that way, there are great achievements!, the worker can even be rented or rented out, I guess not, oh yes, indeed. There is a mistake somewhere, and it's not my doing that one appeared – no two, Jesus, the Lord and inspector Bakunin, it all depends – that now so many others also appeared and can't affect anything either. That's the disadvantage of this net portal. Everybody fits in and all are going through, they run with it and, on the run, everybody picks up valuable information and still, the informations don't get fewer. Everyone is taking something at all times. The portal leads into the land of Cockaigne, no doubt. The more you take, the more regrows. That's all so wonderful now, because in space there is, I already said it, unlimited space. It's not like the Russian doll, you don't have to stuff one into the other, each smaller than the one before until you've got nothing in the end. This space is so spacious no one can put it away anywhere, who would want that anyway, the swipers, not to be confused with sweepers, those who always sweep, would have nothing to swipe and swap any more. This space can't be wiped out any more. It is always there for us, so that we can breathe and go out and still stay at home or wherever we happen to be at the time. Stay where we are. Like the German revolution. Expired,

178

everything. I hereby declare everything null and nothing. Since these net-portals exist, nothing else exists, for they lead into a space, yes, all in one, all for one, which no one can clear any more. Thus I declare everything invalid except for space. I am not saying: this space, or all of you want to go there. There is only the one. There is only one. Any god is nothing compared to it. For example, I declare the following expired: the law, finally, that always equilibrates the relative surplus-population, or industrial reserve army, to the extent and energy of accumulation, this law rivets consumers more firmly to their supermarket than Prometheus with all his pets, the debt-vultures – which however, just like my ravens and wolves can leave any time – to the rock, this is how humans, who have been called consumers for a long time, are riveted to their favourite cosmetics outlet, their favourite drugs store, their favourite brands, their favourite bank branch, to my burst ash branch, my shaft, wherein the contracts are incised, which no one has read in the longest time, even if it were still possible. That law that ever more people mean an ever-increasing army of workers does not apply any more, no law applies any more, but: the law that sooner or later more and more people will come and go does apply, yes, that's correct. Please tick answer 3!, but it rivets the labourer more firmly to capital than Prometheus did, no, not the law, the portal, no, not the portal, the law, since it makes no difference which one, let's say the portal is the law, I mean, that everyone has to get through it, that's the law now, forgive me, I must take Prometheus as an example, because Loge, that Loco, I mean Looki, the one with all his books, is too much, he's never around, he only comes when he is needed, that louch, but he has to be told, and I wouldn't know right now, for what I would need him, well, he's long gone anyway, he was smarter than all of us, that is, firmer, riveting the labourer more firmly to capital, riveting all others as well, to the portal that is, to the portals, there are more of them, after all, they hold up more firmly than the rivets of Mime, of Alberich, of Prometheus, just not together, they don't hang together for the life of them, yes, more firmly riveted is the labourer to capital (and its respective portal) than the screw nuts of Prometheus to the rock. There they come running, the people, they also want to be riveting, no, riveted, if need be also to their jobs. Yes, they would like that best. But they even walk through the net portal, as soon as they have just one minute to spare, they slip through the net of the net and roam about wildly, which they shouldn't do. They should do their jobs and not doo-doo through the portal into something else they won't overlook any more. No one can overlook the open space any more. I made them, humans, but why so many of them? The Panther dances around the fire, he is not the one you seek. Only if you go through this one portal will you see him. But you first will have to find the portal. A short movie is running there so that *you* understand it even better. We made this movie, if you see it *you* will understand us. Whoever doesn't go through it, doesn't see it, that's all. That's why it took so long. *You* know what! That's why the search took so long, because no one came through the portal, no saviour, even though everyone goes through or kicks in so many doors. You will be the one who will be sought, child. By the hero. By only one, who'll come through the fire. Even though it's not a real fire. It is harmless. Anyone could get through, but no one would get the idea. The others get herded together in huge masses, then they are off the street and busy until they have no room anywhere. They no longer go in or out, they just go west. The worker's power grows, albeit into the Nothing, it can grow unlimitedly, but who needs it? The countries sell themselves, but who needs them? The hero's power also grows. In Germany, the worker is no hero and the hero no worker. That's what it all came to. It had to come to that. Only one rules. I? But who needs me? I don't know. Yes, it still is me, but not much longer: fare well, you valiant, glorious child, you, my heart's most hallowed pride, fare well! As you can't ride beside me ever again, lose you I must, whom I love, you, the laughing joy of my eye, a bridal fire will flare up for you such as never blazed for a bride! Fiery flames will encircle the rock, did we have that already? Yes, we did, about the fiery flames, and also about the furnaces on fire, those who work hard would also want food. We already had this. We had everything, patience, I'll stop in a moment, oh well, not so fast. Those who don't work, don't eat, we already had that too. We already had everything. And if *you* go through the net-gate, *you* will find still more than everything. And if there is no radiant, I mean radio mast for the portal, you can spray one for you. There is a spray now, *you* can use it anywhere, wherever *you* are, there just has to be a big vertical surface next to you. No kidding. But *you* can also be that surface for yourself. Why not stand there and spray yourself. Never leave your house alone, always take yourself with you and that spray can, never leave without that vertical surface, on which you can spray your own mast. Bull! Doesn't work, never ever, even though it might sound tempting, well, you might have a ten per cent better reception. Performance: improved by almost ten per cent! Have a try! You will be your own portal then. Your own net portal! Isn't that neat. Can't beat that! One blast from the spray can, and *your* very self is the post in person, I mean, the mast and *you* can even walk through yourself. That's how things stand today, but tomorrow *you* will stand somewhere else, maybe even as the portal, through which others can go, yes, *you* too, of course. Complete BS, invented by the greedy, so that they can cash in real good. There are quite a few other things they did not make up either. And all this for what? Walk right through yourself! *You* must not shun this sensation, don't be shy now! It's not only ghosts one can walk through! No, we don't yet have the hero, he is not available just now, but he'll come. I can promise *you* that. But why do *you* need him at all? So that you don't have to be afraid of one who doesn't know fear, who goes right through *you*, no matter whether or not *you* are one of those human-friendly masts. So that *you* will have someone who does not know fears as *you* have all the time, who takes care of everything for *you* and talks on voicemail without fear, yes, *you* too, with withering fear it frights the faint-hearted, the cowards, they flee, the douche bags, those *Warmduscher*, those milksops, they run, *you* in the midst of them, what did I say? Why then the hero? Power comes from deeds, not words. Enough words. Already far too many words. Thank *you* very much. I knew, *you*'d be blown away. You keep telling me: far too many words, cut! That radiant pair of eyes I often caressed with a smile, when a kiss requited your battle lust, child, when the yearning for hope would sear my heart amidst wildly waving fears. On a happy man their stars shall shine, on the hapless immortal, me, they must close in parting, the fire? The fire that is not one, I just call it that. And thus I, a god, turn away from you. And I go. A spectre haunting around Europe or wherever I shall be. I don't know. I am going. I can go anywhere,

182

can't I? There are no borders. So I go. Smash the machines, who still needs them, and go. Set everything on
fire and go. A German revolution happened in between.
At some time, it was in between, but it could not decide
between whom and what, anyway, it ended like it started, I repeat: those who had the gold, have it again. In
between a small stratum of craftsmen no one needs any
more: liberated!, yes, free at last!, their leader should
also be free, and, why not, the homeless home workers,
who spend their Hartz IV unemployment money so that
they can make everything themselves, in their case,
though, alone. None of it will last, but everyone will be
free. All free. Though I can see it only with this particu-
lar class of workers, I have the metal working industry
in mind and that one is free now; their ring-leader, the
union boss, it's all the same anyway, also free, all free to
go anywhere, like me. This is the revolution: that they
can go anywhere, like a god and stay at home doing so,
or in café-chains, in the net-café, which, however, has
not been used in a long time, because every person is his
own hotspot, everyone is hot and also sports some name
and has his own portal, just that no one is himself any
more, everyone went inside himself or sits with his device in a normal café, since the portal, through which he
has to get is himself, everyone in himself or wherever he
just wants to be at the moment. One post next to the other. The rest is not free, no, all free, the metallers also free
now, and their boss has nothing to do any more either,
doesn't have to jump at us gods with his hate, he is free,
also of property, but with the whole width of the space,
no, not of this space where I am, I am also free, you seek
your own freedom to walk through the portal that is
yourself! You may! We gods ruled by betrayal, it's all
right, no, not all right, I know, but we seemed so mighty

only to the unfree, as unbeatable as their favourite foot-
ball team. Unbeatably strong. But the day before
yesterday Leverkusen clearly overextended itself and
today it's already been three days since they were humiliated, and the days will add up to more ad infinitum.
Doesn't matter. All of them freed by a hero, who shot the
decisive goal. Just that this time it was the others. Many
others also get shot, who cares. I declare the revolution
finished, after all, it also affects me, no, it does not affect
me in the least, I mean it affects not the least in me, I
could just as well declare the revolution opened; property will be like newly distributed, but it only has been
freshly washed, that is, those who had it, have it again
now, exactly, after the hundredth repetition, they finally
got it. It was returned to them, the property. The metallers reached a good deal, their boss is also free now, no
small thing under today's conditions. But the conditions
can change any time again. It can happen very quickly.
One only has to mess them up, like their trash, all the
participants in the revolution, offer them a great con-
cert, good music and they will quickly trample each
other to death and be decimated. Also one of our spe-
cialities, decimating, it comes from the decimal system,
but who is counting? They fight, the people, but they
become fewer and fewer. Fewer and fewer are fighting. I
don't have to do much, but I do whatever is possible. I
scatter and splinter their mass across the whole country,
the hero will know how to help himself, he will also help
those who are in need, he will withstand me, he still
must, notwithstanding his withstanding, die, this will be
called a work of redemption, from his point of view,
whose top disappears in the clouds, no one ever saw it,
his watch-tower, no one ever saw it, not the penthouse
anyway, in any case, no one has seen it in a long time.

Those are the remains of the hero. Yes, down there. Maybe it isn't even him. Maybe it's someone else. Or the hero was something else. Oh, I don't know, I poke around in the ashes, for possibly preserved valuables, bits of possessions, maybe a confession, yes, a ring, I return it, so that conditions, which have been sick, can be restored again and I go. I go online, like everybody, see you! No, I won't see you again. I am not cruising any more. And now I forgot my line. Okay, so I'm going. This net can't hold anyone and doesn't want to either. Everything is boundless, out of bound. Everything restored again? This file, which was sick, restored again? Finally? Good. Before, it wasn't any better either, but also not worse. So then: good. The hero always stands on his own. At that level which I just left, the workers do not fight their enemies, but the enemies of their enemies. They fight blindly, they are not heroes, but they fight. They are still fighting to get to the surface and stay there at least for a few minutes. They just don't see whom they are fighting, no wonder, they don't even want to see it, they want to look at a screen, they just want to play, they want to go, they want to surf where they get trampled just now! Because they stare so stiffly at the screen or the TV, they don't see that they are getting crushed right now. They might possibly see the sole of a shoe, whose they don't know, even though the brand might interest them. What do they care who their enemy is! They are even blinder than I. I still have one eye at least. They no longer have any that would not have been glued, nailed to a screen, available in various sizes from very small to very big, or smashed under sneakers. Losing their own sneakers in the mêlée. They have no eye for anything any more, for nothing. They are in the hands of just a few, they get nothing or very little, they all get it from one hand and it isn't mine. They don't get it from God, I would know that, I am the one who I will become, oh, heck, let's be modest: who I am. They are getting it from just a few and I don't know all of them. Who knows the names? I don't know them. I know a few, but they are the wrong ones. I am going. I don't know anyone any more. I am going. I flush up my ravens, and, lo and behold, they like each other, two of them lifting up the sod, yeah, keep looking, so that the third one who flew in from somewhere, can pick up the seeds underneath. Everyone gets something. They are really nice!, these birds. Using themselves as machines. Not a bad idea. Being their own masters. Nobody uses them in the field. They use one another, and they get the profit from it. I am going. Okay. My daughter says I should look northwards through the night, happy to oblige, but there I don't see anything either. Though it could tempt me, it still could tempt me: yes, goods, yes, God, yes, gold, yes, godly splendour; yes, house, yes, court, yes, imperious pomp, could still tempt me, all of it; rather less could I be tempted in other ways, albeit the family way, maybe not by contracts, not this time, God forbid!, not this time, but everything else, I could be tempted by, yes, love, why not, love. Could tempt me. Everything could tempt me. To the point of white heat that's burning here now, seemingly waiting for something, a hero, a human being, a piece of steel, a can, a second can, made from the first one. With something totally different inside. Let's see, what will become of it.

Richard Wagner, *The Ring of the Nibelung*, Libretto
Richard Wagner, *The Ring of the Nibelung*, Prosaentwurf
Wolfgang Schild, *Staatsdämmerung: Zu Richard Wagner's*
Der Ring des Nibelungen [Nationdämmerung: Richard
Wagner's *The Ring of the Nibelung*]
Karl Marx, *Capital*
Karl Marx and Friedrich Engels, *The Communist Manifesto*
Some Sigmund Freud, but I don't remember what.
Felix Doleke, *Analyse einer Getränkedose zur Abschätzung des
Energiebedarfs bei ihrer Herstellung (Facharbeit)* [Analysis of a
drink can to estimate the energy requirement for its
production (Research paper)]
Herrmann Jelinek, *Kritische Geschichte der Wiener Revolution,
vom 13. März bis zum konstituierenden Reichstag (Wien 1848)*
[Critical History of the Vienna Revolution from 13 March
to the National Diet (Vienna 1848)]
Nothing else. Several newspapers. All nothing.

rein GOLD was written at the suggestion of the Bayerische
Staatsoper, Munich.

Notes from the translator

p22 *malcontents in Zwickau*: The National Socialist
Underground, a cell of German neo-Nazi terrorists,
co-founded by Beate Zschäpe (b. 1975), Uwe Mundlos
(1973-2011) and Uwe Boehnhardt (1977-2011). They are
first introduced in the essay as 'malcontents in Zwickau',
two men and a woman, a post-Communist unholy trinity.
Between 2000 and 2011 the trio was responsible for the
assassinations of nine migrants and a policewoman, two
bombing attacks as well as several bank robberies. They
shared an apartment in the town of Zwickau, Saxony.
Zschäpe met and fell in love with Mundlos as a teenager at
a neo-Nazi youth organisation, where they later befriended
Boehnhardt with whom she also had a relationship. To the
public, she represented the image of a kind, caring and
efficient Hausfrau to her two housemates.

p35 *I am the one you are looking for*: On 4 November, 2011
Mundlos and Boehnhardt rode their bikes to their last
bank robbery. Afterwards they returned with them to a
trailer they had rented for their escape and parked nearby.
Trailed by the police, they set the trailer on fire and
killed themselves, apparently in a murder-suicide. When
Zschäpe found out about their deaths, she burnt down the
apartment after taking their cats to a neighbour. A few days
after the murder Zschäpe called the police and told them,
'I am the one you are looking for.' The officer replied that
he did not know anything about her. One week later she
turned herself in at the station with her lawyer. Jelinek's
response to Zschäpe's trial, *Das schweigsame Mädchen* [The
Silent Maiden], premiered at the Munich Kammerspiele
in 2014. The trial started in 2013 and ended in 2018 with a
life sentence. At the time of this writing her case has been
moved to the Federal Supreme Court.

p55 *Herrmann Jellinek* (1822-1848): A writer and outspoken journalist in the revolutionary year of 1848, who was executed in Vienna for his impassioned criticism of the conditions of peasants and the working urban poor. Jellinek is a distant relative of Elfriede Jelinek (the variations in spelling are common in Jel(l)inek genealogies), who traces their common roots to a peasant, Georg Jelinek in Hungarian Brod. By meaningful coincidence, the young Richard Wagner engaged himself in the 1848 revolutionary movement. Elfriede Jelinek primarily associates the remote forebear with her kinship to the (Jewish) legacy of liberal thought and activism and its persecution to this day, though in her case not with deadly consequences, but with vicious attacks by conservative media and Austria's far right Freedom Party, whose popular, populist leader, the late Jörg Haider was a frequent target of her scathing criticism. She also satirized him in a short play *Das Lebewohl* [The Farewell].

p62 *The Pink Panther*: Over the years, the NSU trio developed a 'Confessor Video' with doctored scenes from the Sixties cartoon. The fifteen-minute film features the Pink Panther (Paulchen by his German name) proudly demonstrating the group's murders on flip charts, watching actual news clips about their crimes, with graphic pictures as well as conventional headshots of the victims to the soundtrack of Henry Mancini's theme music. A few days after the deaths of Mundlos and Boehnhardt, the video showed up at the offices of several German newspapers, presumably sent by Zschäpe.